Trust *the* Confession

Trust *the* Confession

Disavow Ignorance *for* Personal Freedom

LORENZO D. LEONARD

ELEVATE PRESS

Trust the Confession: Disavow Ignorance for Personal Freedom
Copyright © 2023 Lorenzo D. Leonard
All Rights Reserved.

Cover Photo © valentyn640/Adobe Stock
All rights reserved used with permission.

Pubished by Elevate Press

Print ISBN: 978-1-961065-06-2
Ebook ISBN: 978-1-961065-07-9

PRINTED IN THE UNITED STATES OF AMERICA

DEDICATION

The transformation from a raw manuscript to an intelligible book could not have occurred were it not for the editing, overseeing, and mastery of each chapter's summation performed by Beth Lottig. The support for this book's overall thesis and challenge to be succinct, complete, and rounded in expression of thought was well worth experiencing her instructive process.
Thank you, Beth.

CONTENTS

Such A Time As This

Now is the time to plant seeds
The seeds of *Acceptance*
The seeds of *Empathy*
The seeds of *Forgiveness*
The seeds of *Gratitude*
The seeds of *No Judgment*
The seeds of *Patience*
The seeds of *Peace*
So that the next *Generation* will
blossom and flourish into a new
age giving Life one unto another.
Growing and coming together all
Colors, and shades, and Nationalities.
The next *Generation* will have realized that
all Life is connected and that we are all breathing
the same air in this Life.
We all are one: the *Human Race*.
We do matter to one another.

—Cecilia Canada

We can't do much about the length of our lives,
but we can do plenty about its width and depth.

—Evan Esar

A Revelation

When I was young and naive,

I wanted to change the world

to be more open-minded and receptive

to the needs of others considered different.

Rather than champion levels of division,

thrive to exemplify coalitions of equals.

Lastly, broaden credibility, relevance, and value

to include qualities that characterize intrinsic value.

However, as I have aged, and become less naive,

I have come to realize that I am not that powerful

and vain to change a world that is beyond my control.

The best that I can do is change how I am in this domain

by developing my own personal empowerment.

And with this Herculean effort, I have indeed changed the world.

—Lorenzo D. Leonard

PREFACE

*It's one of the greatest gifts you
can give yourself,
to forgive.*

—*Maya Angelou*

*Success is not measured by what a man accomplishes,
but by the opposition he has encountered and the courage
with which he has maintained the struggle
against overwhelming odds.*

— *Charles Lindbergh*

At first glance, the beginning of the title, *Trust the Confession*, may initially come across as puzzling and lacking transparency. However, the phrase has a profound meaning for the person who has reached a point in their life when an accumulation of distressing experiences related to romantic and platonic relationships has become too evident to ignore. To begin a process of reversing the negative results requires an individual to be willing to undergo a self-administered examination to identify self-serving agendas that played a role in creating unfulfilling experiences. To follow long-standing societal traditions and an entrenched cultivation of encouragement to pursue personal meaning and purpose outside of oneself creates an opportunity for an individual to be victimized by a false narrative.

The misinformation that propels an individual onto the path of victimization has to do with linking personal meaning and purpose with *what* an individual is in terms of external status and possesses materially. When an individual invests emotionally, psychologically, and spiritually in external sources—such as wealth, race, ethnicity, religion, career/job, education, athletics, political affiliation, fashion, romance, gender, sexual orientation, physical beauty, marriage, parenting, and home—to provide them with lasting meaning and purpose, one predictable goal is accomplished. The lack of personal depth, meaning, and purpose is developed, along with an excessive praise exhibited toward an alien source that generates an unsavory affirmation. Achieving this type of endorsement supports embracing the deceptive custom of adapting to the limited perimeters of credibility and relevance—and the fantasy of unfailing.

Both private and non-private relationship clashes become inevitable when power, authority, or prominence are limited and sparse in an individual's life. Linking personal meaning and purpose with *what* an individual is externally and possesses materially runs parallel with others chasing the same false narrative; thus, the inevitable clash. Because the main focus is on achieving credibility, relevance, and value, disturbing competitive exploits become amplified. The stampede of human souls to attain credibility and relevance through limited resources dictates the need to gain an advantage over like-minded souls. When personal meaning and purpose are primarily derived from external sources, the need to create practices of injustice, abuse, discrimination, deception, and intolerance to gain an advantage over another individual or group becomes a necessity.

Commonly, the need to discredit and destroy another person or group also in pursuit of legitimacy is initiated by an individual experiencing limited personal power, authority, or prominence in their lives. Jealousy, envy, and contempt directed toward another individual or group are common occurrences among the impoverished. A person can live amongst immense material riches and be emotionally, psychologically, and spiritually impoverished. The lack of knowledge regarding an individual's quality of being and feeling complete—as revealed through their inherent qualities expressive of substantive character—qualifies as impoverishment. Without this knowledge, it becomes quite easy to fall victim to one's ravaged imagination.

One explicit fact is certain—impoverishment is the motivating source that creates the societal tragedy historically manifested as a symptom. There are no synthetic or manufactured laws that will curtail or resolve symptoms such as random gun violence, indiscriminate killing of children and adults, well-organized oppression, repression regarding the rights of women, systematic revoke of voting rights pertaining to the BIPOC population, denouncing same-sex and interracial marriages, inequitable and low-wage practices, or criminalizing immigrants. As a result of being consumed with a personal desperation to exert power, authority, and dominance, the practices of injustice, cruelty, and partiality prevail. It is customary for a class, gender, race, ethnicity, social body, and religion to discredit and destroy one another from within, as well as to direct this agenda toward a different class, gender, race, ethnicity, social body, and religion. A frequent response for this proclivity is to declare humanity inherently corrupt and sinful, which has been argued over for centuries.

The sub-title to this publication, *Disavow Ignorance for Personal Freedom*, is intended to reach a specific individual. The intent is to reach out to the person ready to move forward from a buildup of distressing experiences pertaining to relationships, both romantic and platonic. The pursuit to achieve personal meaning and purpose through external sources has explicit disadvantages. A system of living that promotes power, authority, and prominence as sustainable means to attain legitimacy also is an advocate for an end game obsessed with animosity and division. This type of system, with its one-dimensional focus to achieve legitimacy, incites an environment to turn against itself with hostile, antagonistic, and menacing behavior.

To begin the process of moving beyond relationships that become engulfed in despair, anguish, and unhappiness will first require accountability. The need to feel admired, appreciated, special, connected, seen, heard, and intimate are all valid emotional and psychological needs. It is also a valid expectation for an individual to experience credibility and relevance as a result of these needs being fulfilled. The expectation is more likely to be fulfilled in a secure and stable manner when, during the developmental years, the education of an individual's inherent qualities of substantive character has been internalized and practiced. This education also provides an individual with an understanding of their wholeness and completeness being derived from attributes comprising their substantive character. However, if this education does not take place during the developmental years, an individual will learn through customary social practices to exclusively count on external and material sources, including relationships, to fulfill valid emotional and psychological needs well into adulthood.

As a result of developing this dependency, one significant problem arises for an individual. The problem that is established by following customary social practices is how to abandon oneself. The neglect generates a lack of acquaintance or ignorance regarding the fundamental qualities that comprise a person's wholeness and totality. Due to a lack of familiarity, characteristics such as autonomy, individuality, virtue, and innate intelligence that equal empowerment are personal assets that an individual grows to distrust. In contrast, a great deal of attention is devoted to attaching one's perception of uniqueness to *what* an individual is with the anticipation of feeling admired, appreciated, special, connected, seen, heard, and intimate by an outside or material source. Personal meaning and purpose are byproducts derived from attaching one's uniqueness to *what* that individual is based on external and material factors.

There is nothing inappropriate when it comes to feeling credible and relevant with respect to *what* an individual is in terms of external and material rankings. As long as the rankings are safeguarded by worthy qualities that comprise *who* that person is inherently, moral and principled development is the prophylactic. When moral and principled development has taken place, autonomy, virtue, uniqueness, and innate intelligence do not perceive limitations as do the impoverished. For these individuals, the playing field of competition simply does not exist. Though the impoverished will routinely attempt to discredit and destroy the empowered, envy, jealousy, and resentment tailgate the individual caught in their own netting of accepted weakness. On the other hand, moral and principled development does not allow a person to define their self-perception by experiences. The strength of character permits a person to know they are more than good or bad—or their experiences—by automatically defaulting to *who* an individual is in terms of qualities comprising their intrinsic value.

The process of reversing the negative results associated with romantic and platonic relationships begins with accountability. Once the process of accountability has been satisfied to an individual's contentment, the time to begin stepping away from pursuing personal legitimacy from outside of oneself has arrived. In its place begins the pursuit of personal meaning and purpose based on one's internal resources. Patience and leniency are important traits to develop along with undergoing this significant personal change. The old saying, "Rome was not built in one day," will need to be petitioned on a number of instances. Letting go of a learned ideology to pursue credibility, relevance, meaning, and purpose from external and material sources will not be an easy task to accomplish in the beginning. However, the consistent reminder of an investment in sources outside of oneself to primarily provide personal legitimacy, and the accumulation of distressing romantic and platonic relationships that followed due to this dependency, will help to develop patience and leniency.

The pursuit of personal meaning and purpose based on one's inherent resources that comprise autonomy, originality, and innate intelligence will also take practice and perseverance. *Disavow the Ignorance* and lack of acquaintance pertaining to the very best attributes an individual brings to their life. This way, a person removes themselves from a crowded field of competitors battling one another for limited and unstable external sources. There is no need to "keep up with the Joneses," be it economic well-being, gender, race, ethnicity, education, social status, or political or religious involvements. This is especially true when acquiring and maintaining the latest and greatest regarding external and material procurements can be here today and gone tomorrow.

To strive for excellence, rather than perfection, can attract a form of impoverishment devoted to concealing its deeply felt wound of imperfection through an investment in being right. The allure is motivated by the discontent with observing autonomy, individuality, and innate intelligence openly exhibited as a sign of empowerment. The goal is to discredit and destroy what is a reminder of bondage to an accepted form of limitation. Strive to be good, and right is consistently proven and justified. Whereas strive to be right, and good is placed in perilous and unjustified positions. Simply put, that which is good will always be right, and that which is right does not necessarily translate into that which is good. Intellectual, emotional, and spiritual impoverishment will argue to its death the previous statement's incorrectness.

Keep in mind there are countless individuals and groups who are not interested in transitioning away from power, authority, and importance as a basis to experience credibility and relevance. Learning about inherent value as a means to experience genuine credibility and relevance is a worthless endeavor that will not overshadow the benefit of being in power and prominent. These same individuals and groups will continue to follow societal expectations and pursue external sources to achieve credibility and relevance because their state of impoverishment is supported. Even though the playing field is crowded with hostile and non-hostile challengers, pursuing legitimacy, economic, gender, racial, educational, and social imbalances benefit their way of life. It is only natural for relationships, romantic and platonic, to be consumed with determining what seat at the table controls the power, authority, and importance.

On the contrary, the opportunity to *disavow ignorance in favor of personal freedom* occurs when an individual can recognize and practice the substantive qualities they distinctively possess that comprise their credibility, relevance, and value. The realization that innate attributes represent honorable character will position an individual to initiate a specific drive to experience personal freedom based on empowerment. And just as important, these attributes are more than capable of providing reliable sources to experience personal fulfillment. It is this process that moves an individual beyond the halfway mark and toward the goal of achieving personal freedom.

It is not the case that relationships and material possessions are unimportant. Relationships and material assets will always be recognized as complementary achievements in support of personal contentment. It is the case that no source outside of an individual should become a primary source of dependency to provide personal fulfillment. The personal contentment being exalted will be founded on credible, legitimate, and stable terms. As a result of this newly established contentment, the rejection of any need to develop a dependency on relationships and material resources to fulfill credibility and relevance is far more than just a minor accomplishment.

The subsequent recognition of oneself lacking the knowledge pertaining to their inherent credibility is a personal disclosure that will prompt another moment of enlightenment. Learning of the various advantages of relying on its qualities to experience legitimacy and relevance is a moment of illumination that elicits the act of liberation. The ability to disavow one's previous state of ignorance is a major step taken toward learning to choose relationships that encourage autonomy and empowerment. Another advantage to relying upon qualities comprising inherent credibility is the capacity to distinguish between individuals primarily interested in establishing relationships of mutual interest versus individuals and groups primarily invested in exploitation. Attaching one's identity and self-worth primarily to economic standing, gender, race, ethnicity, education, occupation, athletics, religious, social, and political affiliations are just camouflages in different formats for exploitation.

When an individual becomes open to accepting the personal challenge to engage in moments of soul-searching to examine how past decisions helped to create the experiences of unfulfillment, the resulting confessions can initiate a reversal of fortune: personal fulfillment. This profound journey can be a beginning for an individual to begin making decisions that support their personal freedom rather than a portfolio consisting of counterproductive dependencies. The self-admission of not knowing how to live one's life based on worthy personal attributes that stand on their own as credible, relevant, and genuine can stimulate the next step. This, linked with following through with the action to live a new and enlightened life, significantly alters a balance of power. When an individual speaks truth to power, balance is the inevitable outcome. Traditional and customary sources—formerly used to achieve credibility and relevance that is interrelated with intellectual, emotional, and spiritual impoverishment—become irrelevant.

It is important to understand that this new journey is a direct antagonist to a system of living structured to train an individual to live one's life based on standards and expectations arising from unpredictable and unreliable sources, such as society, culture, race, ethnicity, religion, and education. Attributes such as innate intelligence, creativity, ingenuity, humility, vigor, courage, and resilience validate genuine personal credibility and relevance. Being attentive, considerate, good, cooperative, and reciprocal toward other people confirms a personal meaning and purpose that is honorable. Unreliable and unpredictable sources are parallel with a lack of contentment. Whereas to live a genuine and authentic life runs parallel to contentment and fulfillment.

—Lorenzo D. Leonard

Chapter 1

TO ANSWER AN OLD QUESTION

*One of the most pathetic aspects of human history
is that every civilization expresses itself most pretentiously,
compounds its partial and universal
values most convincingly,
and claims immortality for its finite
existence at the very moment
when the decay which leads to death has already begun.*
—Reinhold Niebuhr

However vast the darkness, we must supply our own light.
—Stanley Kubrick

One certainty that can be generally agreed upon is that fever, abdominal pain, headache, and fatigue are recognized as symptoms directly related to a specific source. In an even-handed and impartial manner, the intent of this chapter is to address the question of whether or not America is a racist nation. The short answer is absolutely no—America is not a racist nation. The long answer will explain how racism qualifies as a chronic symptom that represents an immense societal impairment. The disorder that motivates racism committed against Black and brown cultures is the same that provokes hate crimes committed against the indigenous people of America, Jews, Asian, and Muslim cultures. It is the identical impairment that induces and breeds chronic symptoms, such as societal inequities, inequalities, injustice, domestic violence, childhood obesity, drug and alcohol addiction, bullying, and depression. The impulse to inflict abuse, cruelty, injustice, or suffering either onto oneself or another is motivated by a long-standing societal impairment.

From the beginning of its existence, humanity has been dominated by an intellectual, emotional, and spiritual impairment, which is outwardly demonstrated as impoverishment. When personal legitimacy is determined by how much power, authority, and prominence an individual or group can acquire, it becomes necessary to create societal inequities, inequalities, and practices of injustice to sustain this form of pseudo-legitimacy. The founding documents of this society were written not to include women, the BIPOC populations, and whites who were not property owners. In the beginning and to this current time period, it was this state of impairment that prevented the American experiment from developing a moral blueprint that included all of its people.

Thomas Paine, an Englishman, emigrated to America and, shortly after his arrival, became widely known throughout the colonies as a political activist, theorist, and philosopher. In January 1776, he published a forty-seven-page pamphlet that was a huge success in America and Europe. Over 150,000 copies of Paine's first printing sold out in just two weeks. The title of his pamphlet was *Common Sense*, which became a robust voice in favor of revolutionary causes in America and Europe. Thomas Paine's *Common Sense* could easily be mistaken as a document that was meant to include all of America's people. The moral blueprint stood at the door of America's outset. In *Rights of Man* and *Common Sense*, Thomas Paine said an individual's duty is to allow the same rights to others as we allow ourselves.[1] The failure to do so causes the creation of a social issue.

Had it not been for Founding Father John Adams, the second president of the United States (1797–1801) and the first vice president under President George Washington, the creation of social issues that are based on the flexing of power, authority, and importance may have had a different look throughout this nation's history. Thomas Paine's *Common Sense* was a "disastrous meteor." Paine's inflammatory call for independence would undermine the deliberative (calculated) work of the Continental Congress. Adams stated, "I dreaded the effect so popular a pamphlet might have among the people and determined to do all in my power to counteract the effect of it." Adams felt Paine "went much further and wrote with driving incendiary prose. Condemn monarchy, embrace democracy, and inspire the world." Paine insisted, "We have it in our power to begin the world all over again." With this, Adams stated, "Paine's plan was so democratically (popularly), without any restraint or even an attempt at any equilibrium or counterpoise, that it must produce confusion and every evil work."[2]

No, America is not a racist nation, but it is and has been dominated by moral impoverishment. This form of impoverishment is

---

[1] Marianne Garvey, "What Are the Examples of Social Issue and How It Affects You?" *VentureJolt*, October 21, 2022, https://venturejolt.com/2022/10/21/example-of-social-issue/.

[2] "John Adams on Thomas Paine's Common Sense," *Making the Revolution: America, 1763–1791*, Primary Source Collection, National Humanities Center, https://americainclass.org/sources/makingrevolution/rebellion/text7/adamscommonsense.pdf.

the fertile ground that supports the growth of hate, prejudice, discrimination, and resentment directed against an individual or group of people on the basis of race or ethnicity. John Adams, Thomas Jefferson, George Washington, James Madison, and other Founding Fathers were highly shrewd, politically perceptive, and vastly educated men. However, when establishing this American experiment, the primary commitment of the Founding Fathers was to protect their wealth and prominent status.

Denying women, the BIPOC population, and poor white people voting rights helped to safeguard their positions of privilege and entitlement. The secondary commitment of the Founding Fathers was to establish a system of living similar to what they were familiar with—a way of life based on power, authority, and importance. The Founding Father's agenda was at the expense of denying all Americans to "have it in our power to begin the world all over again."[3] Personal empowerment was considered too democratic and too much of a gamble. Even though *too democratic* would have been a vast improvement from the economic, political, and religious tyranny previously experienced in England, the distinct prospect of a balance of power was simply out of the question.

The personal pursuit of power, authority, and prominence to achieve legitimacy can deposit a great deal of chronic symptoms across the playing field of competition. This deposit manages to exist because the education to identify qualities that comprise a person's core intrinsic value lacks a societal demand to include such a curriculum into its way of life. Therefore, victims are aplenty across the playing field because of an individual's inability to separate intellectually, emotionally, and spiritually from experiences that involve

---

[3] Laksiri Fernando, "First Appreciation of Thomas Paine and His *Common Sense*," *Colombo Telegraph*, April 6, 2017, https://www.colombotelegraph.com/index.php/first-appreciation-of-thomas-paine-his-common-sense/.

chronic symptoms. The system of living this society has chosen to adopt from its beginning as a tradition to achieve credibility and relevance creates an arranged set of circumstances that allow long-term symptoms to dominate the American way of life. For example, hate crimes, random gun violence, the blanket killing of children and adults, oppression and repression regarding the rights of women, systematic revoke of voting rights pertaining to the BIPOC population, decrying same-sex and interracial marriages, inequitable and low-wage practices, and criminalizing immigrants have become normalized.

As to this nation's system of living, there is one shatterproof feature that has successfully survived throughout America's existence. What has helped guarantee this feature's survival is its primary function. Historically, this feature has been sheltered from collapsing because a vast number of individuals and groups, from the most powerful to the least powerful, act in agreement to honor this specific feature. It is absolutely necessary to safeguard the feature's pretense for achieving credibility, relevance, and value. With power, authority, and dominance linked with the massing of material resources and economic wealth, deceit and corruption are ever-present. This feature's main purpose is to protect the actions of power, authority, and dominance when exceeding limits of morality to initiate a chronic societal symptom, such as inequality, inequity, injustice, or acts of cruelty.

As previously stated, America's system of living is as old as humanity, where power, authority, and prominence are equated with credibility and relevance. This system has incorporated into its way of life a distractive strategy. This feature is necessary in order to maintain a priority over ambitions that focus solely on *what* an individual is externally and materially possesses versus support for personal empowerment that recognizes *who* an individual is based on substantive character. This specific feature has been cleverly designed to persuade an individual or group to participate in conceiving solutions and creating laws that nonsensically do nothing more than keep alive the chronic symptoms that morally plague society. Educate to the inherent qualities comprising substantive character, and the chronic symptoms that immorally plague society dissipate. They dissolve because hearts and minds are charged rather than simply seeking to alter behavior through developing nonsensical and superfluous laws. The "more things change, the more they remain the same," as a vast number of individuals and groups, from the most powerful to the least powerful, continue to honor the aforementioned feature: the pretense of credibility and relevance based on power, authority, and prominence.

Again, the initial focus here is not directed toward any particular individual, economic structure, social construct, race, ethnicity, or religion. However, the focus is directed toward an embedded, unprincipled system of living that generates a counterproductive and absurd reality for humanity. Solving the problem of intellectual, emotional, and spiritual impoverishment begins with understanding a solution cannot be attained by shielding its existence with a continuation of a familiar narrative. To do so only protects a system of living dominated by the abusive use of power, authority, and prominence. Apart from the exceptional forms of the unassailable attributes exhibited due to character development, there are no manufactured laws that will curtail or dissolve the habitual forms of chronic and distractive symptoms that morally corrupt this nation.

It is correct to assume that any system of living—government, culture, race, ethnicity, religion, family—that inspires a person to ignore and turn away from their inherent legitimacy has a negative agenda in mind to implement. In its place, there is encouragement to embrace external resources as a means to primarily attain credibility and relevance, which, at this point, translates into a predictable outcome. The prospect of that person being manipulated by external sources for the benefit of attaining power, authority, and importance is greatly bolstered. The ability to *disavow ignorance for personal freedom* is diminished when there is a deficiency in terms of understanding the attributes comprising one's inherent strengths.

And any system of living that neglects to establish a curriculum to educate a person to recognize, value, and practice the best attributes they humanly possess clearly demonstrates that negative agenda. This strategy's end goal is to depict the development of a personal moral blueprint as a sign of weakness and limitation. In its place, thoughts based on impoverishment, power, authority, and prominence are depicted as ultimate signs of invincibility. This type of system becomes a leading antagonist against an individual or group accepting and practicing a personal truth that expresses their all-inclusive value. And that personal truth includes both *who* a person is intrinsically and, to a slightly less degree of importance, *what* a person is externally.

The media, journalists, scholars, educators, and numerous laypersons never quite get to a place where they can adequately and competently explain the root cause of society's historic and contemporary chronic distractive symptoms. Countless interviews, articles, and commentaries are devoted to describing the human carnage headlining that specific day's distractive symptoms, victimized by the impoverished. The inability or reluctance to investigate the root cause for the reoccurring symptoms of inequality, inequity, and cruelty is primarily due to the respective evaluators' personal investment in maintaining the existing state of affairs. It is difficult to skillfully probe a modus operandi based on the successful attainment of power, authority, and prominence while having achieved that goal. When personal meaning and purpose are primarily derived from external sources, the need to protect practices of injustice, inequality, inequity, and deception by avoiding going below the surface becomes a necessity.

Again, the question begs to be asked: Is America a racist, gender, class, and socially oppressive nation? To efficiently answer the question requires a deep dive into the early history of global civilization, which we will cover at length in Chapter 2

Chapter 2

THE FOUNDATION FOR THE OLD QUESTION

If you are distressed by anything external,
the pain is not due to the thing itself,
but to your estimate of it.
—Marcus Aurelius

A true friend is a single soul dwelling in two bodies.
—Aristotle

From a historical frame of reference, as far back as over 3,000 years ago, some astute and wise writers used allegories to portray human experiences relative to their way of life. What is of importance is how ancient allegories continue to be relevant during contemporary times. For example, when reading specific allegories written during ancient civilizations, the reader is exposed to language, such as *goddess* and *god*. Power, authority, and dominance easily come to mind in association with these terms. The same association comes to mind during contemporary times as men and women attempt to reach the status of goddess and god through beauty, wealth, and prominence.

The opportunity to explore civilization's earliest history in association with its allegories provides the chance to closely estimate when humanity's onset with impoverishment may have originated. It was not uncommon for myths to have been created and passed down generations earlier through oral traditions. So, it is a high probability the onset of impoverishment began generations earlier before writing came into existence. What can be safely assumed prior to the existence of writing are systems of living that lacked interest in assisting people in empowering themselves with the knowledge of their inherent credibility.

With the advent of goddesses and gods to worship, the altruistic goal to encourage and support a populace to embrace their own inherent credibility would declare their obsolescence. What emerges from this exploration is how the use of specific allegories inscribed by astute and wise writers highlighted this deficiency. Lacking the knowledge of attributes comprising inherent credibility became an easy pathway to be distracted with cultivating an obsession with solving symptoms rather than the problem. In humanity's infancy, the attention given to recognizing power, authority, and dominance as definitive forms of credibility and relevance impeded its moral growth. Over 3,000 years later, this same goal of impeding civilization's moral growth can be observed in contemporary times.

It is important to mention the contribution academia has made to the reconstruction of ancient myths by rendering from one language into another to better understand interrelated conditions. Philip Joseph Zuckerman, PhD, a professor of sociology and secular studies at Pitzer College in Claremont, California, clarifies when the early allegories were initially written. Zuckerman also specializes in the sociology of substantial secularity. In his *Psychology Today* blog entitled "Before Adam and Eve: Myths and American Consciousness,"

Zuckerman takes the opportunity to expand the thinking of his audience by revealing allegories that involve the ancient Sumerian couple of Inanna and Dumuzi. The metaphors he discloses occurred prior to the Adam and Eve metaphor located in the first book of the Hebrew Bible and the Christian Old Testament.

Zuckerman states:

> The story of Adam and Eve was not the first story of the first humans, as many Americans falsely think. There were many stories about many people long before Adam and Eve. And furthermore, it is obvious that whoever wrote the story of Adam and Eve was influenced by some key details from the preexisting Middle Eastern story of Inanna and Dumuzi.

Myths are wonderful things: they reveal deep truths about the human experience. They affirm values, broaden imaginations, and offer ways for us to reflect upon our choices, mistakes, foibles, passions, and aspirations. And they're simply great stories.[4]

To understand the starting point when civilization began to embrace moral impoverishment as a practical way of life, it is important to consider Zuckerman's statement and go beyond the 1500 BCE written metaphor of Adam and Eve. It is also important to examine the three major allegories that involve Inanna and Dumuzi. "The Courtship of Inanna & Dumuzi," "Dumuzi's Dream," and "Inanna's Descent to the Underworld" were written 500 years earlier, around 2000 BCE. This exploration confirms the lack of recognition and

---

[4] Phil Zuckerman, PhD, "Before Adam and Eve," *Psychology Today*, April 19, 2017, https://www.psychologytoday.com/us/blog/the-secular-life/201704/adam-and-eve.

value accorded to an individual's innocence that comprises the attributes representative of inherent credibility. Generations later, the Adam and Eve metaphor would confirm humanity's acceptance of power, authority, and dominance as a means of achieving credibility and relevance through the exploitation of self-will. Instead of accepting one's innocence as a pathway to embrace personal empowerment, self-importance and self-indulgence would provide an individual with allegedly more control over their destiny.

Samuel Noah Kramer and Diane Wolkstein coauthored the book *Inanna, Queen of Heaven and Earth: Her Stories and Hymns From Sumer*. The significance of the discoveries contained within this book cannot be overstated, as well as two decisive elements that arise from its content. One such element is described by the former Romanian historian of religion, fiction writer, philosopher, and professor at the University of Chicago, Mircea Eliade. He states: "With the publication of this book, we have for the first time in any modern literary form one of the most vital of ancient myths—that of Inanna (known to the Semites as Ishtar), the world's first goddess of recorded history and the beloved deity of the ancient Sumerians." There can be no denial as to the prominence Mircea Eliade bestows upon this masterpiece of literary work. Neither can there be any diminished prominence of this work, as affirmed by Kramer regarding Wolkstein and his work on this project. He states:

This book is a graphic example of an effective cooperation between two specialists working in contrasting, yet complementary, areas of humanistic research: a folklorist who has collected and recorded the tales, legends, and songs of modern contemporary societies, and a cuneiform still who has devoted his entire scholarly career to the restoration and translation of the written tales, legends, and songs of the ancient Sumerians. The Sumerian tales, legends, and songs are part of a vast literature inscribed on clay tablets and fragments scattered throughout museums the world over. There are contents which date back to 2000 BC.[5]

This widespread theme regarding the significance of culture began with the Sumerian (Sumer), which is considered the oldest civilization in the world. The Goddess Inanna and, to a lesser degree, the God Dumuzi are considered the originators when this importance came into existence by way of the written word. Kramer reinforces this magnitude by stating: "Female deities were worshipped and adored all through Sumerian history. But the goddess who outweighed, overshadowed, and outlasted them all was a deity known to the Sumerians by the name of Inanna, Queen of Heaven and Earth. Inanna played a greater role in myth, epic, and hymn than any other deity, male or female."[6]

Diane Wolkstein provides an analysis that summarizes the Inanna intrigue.

> In the "Cycle of Inanna" in "The Huluppu-Tree," she appears to us as a young woman in search of her womanhood. In "Inanna and the God of Wisdom," she achieves her queenship. In "The Courtship of Inanna and Dumuzi," she chooses the shepherd Dumuzi to be her lover, her husband, and the King of Sumer. In "The Descent of Inanna," Inanna leaves for the underworld and is allowed to return from the Great Below only on the condition that she choose a substitute (which is her husband, Dumuzi). In the last

---

[5] Diane Wolkstein and Samuel Noah Kramer, *Inanna, Queen of Heaven and Earth: Her Stories and Hymns from Sumer* (New York: Harper & Row, 1983), xiii.

[6] Wolkstein and Kramer, *Inanna*, xv.

section of the cycle, the "Seven Hymns to Inanna," Inanna is greeted and loved in many aspects. The world's first love story, two thousand years older than the Bible—tender, erotic, shocking, and compassionate—is more than a momentary entertainment. It is a sacred story that has the intention of bringing its audience to a new spiritual place. With Inanna, we enter the place of exploration: the place where not all energies have been tamed or ordered.[7]

Just concluded is a discussion pertaining to one of two elements that could not be overstated, mentioned earlier, involving the importance of discoveries included in Kramer and Wolkstein's coauthored book. However, the second element has been overshadowed by the "pomp and circumstance" devoted to the ancient discoveries in their book. Yet it is the second element revealed throughout the allegories that uncovers a foundation representing the immoral blueprint humanity has historically adopted as a way of life. The blueprint answers the question as to why humanity has accepted moral impoverishment as a viable way of life to adopt, knowing of its self-inflicted adverse impact.

The second element pertaining to the Sumerian discoveries received no attention from Philip Joseph Zuckerman, PhD, Mircea Eliade, Samuel Noah Kramer, and Diane Wolkstein. This distinctive feature is just as significant, if not more than the first element. What the researchers failed to notice was the same process that takes place once a person enters this life in modern times emerges as a common theme throughout the Inanna allegories. Not long after arrival, the first self-inflicted injury a person learns to adjust to is how to deceive oneself through a process that cultivates self-betrayal.

---

[7] Wolkstein and Kramer, *Inanna*, xviii.

- 14 -

This subtle, self-inflicted exploit initiates the development of intellectual, emotional, and spiritual impoverishment. Training to reject the best qualities an individual brings with them into this life is a well-established custom that becomes the earliest experience with accepting two chronic symptoms that become integrated into their way of life. The two chronic symptoms that become well-established behaviors are self-betrayal and the act of betrayal with respect to relationships. The negative impact from this training is to develop a dislike, hostility, fear, and nervousness when in the presence of authenticity and accountability relative to relationships.

Unless the inherent attributes that characterize an individual's completeness are valued and practiced, in its place, betrayal and corruption become an established state of mind. When inherent traits—such as virtue, innate intelligence, creativity, fairness, community, compassion, thoughtfulness, authenticity, and autonomy—are ignored as being inconsequential, this is an act of self-betrayal. At this precise moment, an individual's unrecognized moral blueprint becomes a casualty to impoverishment. When external sources, such as economic and social prominence, profession, gender, race, ethnicity, religion, physical strength, sensuality, and beauty, are considered more compelling as a means to attain legitimacy, this will initiate the act of corruption.

Power, authority, and dominance will be necessary to use in the forms of discrimination, injustice, and cruelty to retain a position of supremacy over competitors who are also in pursuit of this identical legitimacy. History is full of examples regarding the collapse of civilizations, governments, and political, social, and religious institutions due to a person's inherent credibility being considered less significant than a person's external credibility. The Roman, British, Japanese, Spanish, Russian, and Mongol Empires eventually collapsed, mainly due to an inability to balance a way of life dominated by immorality with moral doctrines. Placing the focus on recognizing and practicing inherent credibility initiates the development of substantive character, whereas a principle focus on recognizing external credibility and relevance initiates the dangerous games of betrayal and corruption. Any system of living, whether a collective or individual effort that encourages power, authority, and dominance to sustain self-importance and self-indulgence, establishes a state of intellectual, emotional, and spiritual impoverishment.

Helping to lead the way for self-interest to be successful are the traits of deception, disloyalty, and dishonesty. It is not surprising how acts of betrayal and corruption become customary occurrences when relationships are structured on power, authority, and prominence. This same system refuses to educate its populace to value and practice inherent credibility because this teaching leads to the acceptance of an individual's wholeness and completeness. Teachings of this magnitude would be a direct threat to the persistent reminder that an individual's gateway to personal contentment is through external and material sources. To supplement this erroneous teaching is another flawed training. To fall short of this conquest confirms the existence of lack that confirms a person's incompleteness.

Even though Inanna eventually achieves her queenship in "Inanna and the God of Wisdom," the experience is one of agitation, anger, and chaos. While she and the God of Wisdom, Enki, continuously consume an alcoholic beverage, he passes onto Inanna attributes considered necessary to fulfill her role as Queen of Heaven. Many of the attributes representing her "spiritual heritage" were linked to power, authority, domination, and sexual, sensual, and religious depictions. The depictions included a dagger, sword, the destruction of cities, falsehood, enmity, the art of prostitution, slanderous speech, power, treachery, fear, dismay, and deceit. Inanna also received attributes that, if recognized and practiced, would provide the opportunity to claim her inherent credibility and experience an empowerment not linked to power, authority, domination, and sexual, sensual, and religious expressions. She received truth, the art of forthright speech, heroship, victory, adoring speech, the rejoicing of the heart, the art of kindness, and the perceptive ear.

After receiving the gifts of "spiritual heritage," Inanna leaves the God of Wisdom. As the effect of the alcohol begins to dissipate, Enki becomes angry and upset after realizing that he has passed on to Inanna far more attributes than necessary. He realizes she now possesses all the power, authority, and domination to rule as a full-fledged Queen of Heaven and Earth. Enki makes several attempts to retrieve the gifts but to no avail. He even sends his devoted servant Isimud in these attempts to take back the gifts. From Kramer and Wolkstein's *Inanna, Queen of Heaven and Earth,* Inanna stands firm against her father. Betrayal and deceit will not be received well.

She states to Isimud after the initial attempt to have the gifts returned:

> My father has changed his word to me! He has violated his pledge—broken his promise! Deceitfully my father spoke to me! Deceitfully he cried: 'In the name of my power! In the name of my holy shrine!' Deceitfully he sent you to me![8]

The God of Wisdom, Enki, finally surrenders to Inanna's persistence to keep the gifts of "spiritual heritage" and quickly realizes he now has become the patriarch of a daughter who has become a

---

[8] "Inanna and the God of Wisdom," *Inanna and Dumuzi blog.* https://inannadumuzi.wordpress.com/inanna-and-the-huluppu-tree/.

prevalent and deep-rooted deity. In the restricted role as a God of Wisdom, "Enki can have no hold over her."[9] Because there is an absence of a cultural curriculum that educates an individual to value and practice their inherent qualities indicative of personal wholeness, the gifts of a presumed "spiritual heritage" are limited to the recognition of external distinctions. "The Courtship of Inanna and Dumuzi" was a classic example of a focus on external distinctions as credible and relevant. To secure the goddess's love, the courtship was primarily centered around the shepherd's resolve to outclass a competitive local farmer with gifts and promises to please and accommodate the deity.

The goddess's external beauty, sensuality, proficiency at seduction, and openly expressed statements pertaining to sex would be the path for the shepherd to personally feel whole and complete. The separate acts of self-betrayal by both Inanna and Dumuzi would be how the courtship began with a principal emphasis on *what* each other is and brings to the relationship rather than the essence of *who* they are intrinsically. Prior to the marriage, Inanna and Dumuzi's relationship could be described as basically sultrily, sexually blissful, euphoric, overpowering, and fierce. The subsequent marriage was not without turmoil, which began with Dumuzi pressuring Inanna shortly after the honeymoon to "let me go, sister, let me go."

When recognition, value, and practice of attributes such as nurturance, modesty, sensitivity, compassion, leadership, strength, courage, and independence remain lacking, this vacuum will subsequently be filled with contrary traits, hence the attraction to the dark side or underworld where intellectual, emotional, and spiritual impoverishment is the harvest. In that instant, an individual's moral blueprint becomes a casualty to impoverishment. Betrayal presents

---

[9] Wolkstein and Kramer, *Inanna*, 149.

itself when the vacuum reserved for thoughtfulness and forgiveness is filled with contempt, hatred, and self-loathing.

Examining the beginning of civilization's first recorded written history answers the question of whether America is a racist nation. The response to the question remains no. The mythical story of Inanna is full of examples concerning self-betrayal, which is the first building block for the existence of impoverishment. As previously stated, Inanna is unaware of the inherent qualities that comprise her personal wholeness. Instead, credibility and relevance are based on *what* she is externally as a goddess of war, her sexuality, fertility, and passion for physical love. Racism in America is based on a similar credibility and relevance to determine legitimacy. There is an unawareness regarding inherent qualities comprising authentic credibility and relevance, which is meticulously dwarfed by the limited recognition of external distinctions, such as Caucasian and BIPOC.

At the beginning of recorded history, women recognized they possessed credible gifts relative to their body that could be employed to help the male to feel personally adored, purposeful, and complete. Accepting this position of leverage elevated their positions of power, authority, and prominence. Man, at the start of recorded history, was far too willing to oblige her this power, authority, and domination: hence, the distinction between goddess and god. Gender inequality became quite apparent during ancient times and continues to exist in the modern era. During this first recorded history regarding civilization, women were considered the center of life when taking into consideration their reproductive process, sensuality, and sexual pleasure. Mythology portrayed men as gods in a lesser position of power, authority, and dominance than female goddesses.

Gender inequality certainly existed in favor of the woman as a goddess of beauty, sensuality, and sex, which gave her power, authority, and dominance over her male counterpart. This would dramatically change, however, with the Amorite King Hammurabi during the rise of the Babylonian civilization. Women would be removed as goddesses of beauty, sensuality, and sex by laws that protected men from their own weakness for being physically loved and cherished. Because the genuine experience of feeling loved, cherished, and valued based on inherent qualities of merit was lacking, impoverishment would raise its ugly head. Man would eventually work to overturn this imbalance to protect himself from his longing and weakness for being loved with an all-out attempt to reverse the balance of power, authority, and domination in his favor.

Inanna's durability as a goddess would survive for several centuries and seven name changes until the eventual collapse of the Sumerian civilization in approximately 1750 BCE with the invasion of the region by the Elamites. The ancient culture, Elam, was conquered by the Amorite King Hammurabi during the rise of the Babylonian civilization. Shortly after the Sumerian collapse came the insertion of male deities into the province of worship. By Hammurabi's reign in 1792 BCE, even though Inanna's legacy somewhat persisted, female goddesses had been replaced by male gods.

Clearly, femininity has always been an integral part of religion and, indeed, of civilization; many scholars have argued that the world's earliest societies were matriarchal. So how did we get from all these goddesses and women-inclusive faiths to the rise of monotheistic, patriarchal faiths like traditional Islam, Christianity, and Judaism? We can safely guess that there was a connection between the demonization of pagan and polytheistic faiths and the subjugation and minimization of women.[10]

---

[10] Michael Delahoyde, "Ancient Goddess Religions," Washington State University, https://public.wsu.edu/~delahoyd/mythology/goddess.html.

In her academic treatise titled 1750, Hammurabian Dynasty, Babylon, Ishtar, and Inanna, Joan Eahr—an author, fieldwork director, archivist of open access Re-Genesis Encyclopedia, alum and adjunct faculty at California Institute of Integral Studies—describes the shift from female deities to male deities. Eahr states:

> In the Hammurabian Dynasty, the northern cities of Mesopotamia fell to the Babylonian army led by Hammurabi 1792–1750). In conjunction with this defeat was the introduction of the Hammurabi Laws that replaced former marriage laws. (The Hammurabi code of laws, a collection of 282 rules, established standards for commercial interactions and set fines and punishments to meet the requirements of justice.) Previous to the Codex of Hammurabi, the domicile of the husband and wife (consort/partner?) was in the home of the wife's family. This matrilocal arrangement was known as a beena marriage. In the beena marriage, women had divorce rights plus certain other rights and autonomy. Patrilocal marriage laws were formalized in which female rights and autonomy were abrogated.

> Restricting female attire dates back to the Codes of Hammurabi and continues in the twenty-first century throughout much of the Middle East. With the rise of a new economic order through trade and the appearance of skills and specialties associated with the rise of a military class, the social conditions were created in which biological paternity and the inheritance of private property could become culturally recognized and socially institutionalized. It may not have happened

overnight, but it was a revolution, nonetheless. The world by the end of the second millennium was a man's world, above and below: and the ancient goddesses have all but disappeared. Man cut the umbilical cord to the Great Mother with a sword, and the sword n hanging over his head ever since.[11]

The dominant theme arising from the review of the second element in relation to the Sumerian allegories is the ever-presence of either self-betrayal or betrayal initiated from an external source. Because scholars were focused on their specific agenda, identifying the commencement of behavior that has independently undermined humanity's existence eluded detection. All told, it is a behavior that has set humanity in opposition and conflict with one another for centuries. Throughout the course of the contemporary era, it is troubling to report there are no signs of hope on the horizon for reversing this pattern of navigating across relationships. The basis for the existence of betrayal is due to a lack of understanding of one's inherent credibility, strengthened later by denial, and finally fortified by the ultimate rejection of one's intrinsic value. The act of betrayal formulated in this manner symbolizes intellectual, emotional, and spiritual impoverishment.

For countless centuries, the omission of teachings supporting character development that would distinguish the difference between empowerment and power has been continuously supported by various factions within the human race for one explicit reason. Hierarchal institutions such as government, judicial, commerce, religion, military, political, family, racial, ethnic, and educational structures have engaged in a common agenda. The shared strategy is to continue

---

[11] Joan Eahr, "1750, Hammurabian Dynasty, Babylon, Ishtar, and Inanna," *Academia.edu*, Retrieved December 19, 2022, from https://www.academia.edu/36576533/129_1750_Hammurabian_Dynasty_Babylon_Ishtar_and_Inanna_pdf.

striving to maintain positions of power, authority, and prominence that would preserve the hierarchal structure. The intent behind this repressive agenda of omission is to keep as many of the populace ignorant of personal qualities that would illuminate a moral blueprint spearheaded by autonomy, individuality, and self-confidence based on inherent credibility.

To fall short of accomplishing this repressive agenda would encourage an upsurge of moral blueprints amongst the populace. Success with developing autonomy, individuality, and self-confidence based on inherent credibility is a direct threat to legitimacy determined by power, authority, and prominence. This pathway to personal wholeness and freedom convinces an individual to view oneself on equal footing with other human inhabitants. Equality is recognized no matter the economic, professional, social, or religious status of the other person. Reliance on internal qualities that represent authenticity is an enduring form of credibility, rather than yielding to enticing, unstable, and deceptive attractions to primarily rely on external credibility.

The second intent of the repressive agenda regarding the omission of teachings relative to character development is to protect against the discontinuance of betrayal's negative appeal. Self-betrayal frequently follows acceptance of the unreliable and deceptive attractions associated with primarily pursuing external credibility for personal legitimacy. The motivation to pursue this form of credibility is energized by an internal state of impoverishment that later cultivates the act of betrayal within the relationship. Unless the inherent attributes that represent a person's wholeness are valued and practiced, in its place, betrayal and corruption are accepted behaviors that promote a false assumption concerning an individual's totality.

This scenario took place during the Sumerian timeline, and it certainly took place after its collapse. The origins of injustice, discrimination, cruelty, or antagonism based on gender, class, race, ethnicity, religion, education, and age were rooted in a system of living at the beginning of mythical literature. Different symptoms representing various forms of oppression were exhibited throughout this early history. Beginning with Inanna and her complete focus on *what* she was, rather than a combination that would include reputable attributes representing *who* she was, innately established a historically indisputable act of self-betrayal. To this moment in contemporary history, factions of humanity have yet to learn very little with respect to qualities comprising their innate credibility. To rationalize the presence of this vacuum, a number of atheist, agnostic, and religious advocates hold to the notion that humanity enters this life at birth morally corrupt. To maintain this viewpoint would explain why factions of humankind have a propensity to develop appetites for injustice, discrimination, and cruelty.

Generations after the Inanna allegories exposed the early presence of betrayal, astute and wise writers experienced the same immoral underpinning characterized as betrayal within their system of living. This acute and chronic symptom, which reveals itself not too long after birth, was witnessed by these observant writers. It is not difficult to understand how this social dilemma entailing acts of betrayal and its adverse impact on their way of life could be an incentive to write the Adam and Eve metaphor. Both the Inanna and the Huluppu-Tree and Adam and Eve metaphors took place in the Middle East with a tree as an important symbol of life. Both metaphors involve a man and a woman, a sacred garden, a depraved serpent with an agenda to discredit and/or destroy, and, most of all, acts of betrayal.

Wishing for the vanishing of impoverishment and its attempts to diminish and/or extinguish it is nothing more than excessive vanity. This is explicitly true when lacking personal responsibility to develop one's own moral blueprint that will eliminate conscious or unconscious cooperation. Inanna is not cognizant of the confession that can initiate the transformation of her espoused blueprint of power, authority, and prominence into a morally based blueprint. The confession that she does not know how to live her life based on innate characteristics that endorse her genuine credibility and relevance is the revelation that can lead to personal freedom. This emancipation begins with an acceptance of innate qualities that exemplify principled character and generate personal empowerment—replacing a way of life that promotes self-betrayal and attracts betrayal from external sources. To submit to this substitution is an experience that is the opposite of excessive vanity.

However, due to Inanna's lack of knowledge pertaining to her genuine value, the evil serpent, the fearsome and contrary lion-headed eagle, and the dark demonic female figure remain as her hostile companions. The self-betrayal becomes even more distinct when Inanna ultimately submits to a common scheme often used when a person is faced with the dismal consequences that stem from making harmful personal choices. Inanna pursues outside sources to rescue her from the negative and destructive influences her hostile companions are exerting with respect to transforming the coveted tree into her "shining throne and luscious bed." The common scheme Inanna employs is to be liberated from her impoverished companions while maintaining her impoverished state of mind. The thirst to exert more external power, authority, and prominence will temporarily solve her need for self-contentment.

When comparing pathways to attaining power, authority, and prominence for both the oldest and current civilizations, there is no difference. The lack of a social curriculum to educate a populace to recognize and value inherent credibility comprised of attributes that represent substantive character, autonomy, and personal empowerment are similarities for both civilizations. As a result of this deficiency, personal ambitions are limited to choices solely associated with external sources. Because the exploit is confined to cultivating *what* a person is regarding their external status and material sources, advancing self-importance becomes an individual's core concern. This concern can be witnessed as credibility and relevance are inclined to be outwardly expressed with the intention to persuade or impress.

As previously stated, America's system of living supports gender inequality, racism, and other discriminatory practices. Its system of living is as old as humanity, where power, authority, and prominence are equated with credibility and relevance. As long as personal legitimacy is gauged by the accumulation of any one or a combination of the three determinants, self-betrayal and the act of betrayal plays an active role in determining the tension, inflexibility, and lack of trust with respect to relationships. Also incorporated into this system of living is a strategy to maintain an inflated level of importance and relevance pertaining to personal ambitions that focus on achieving a rank or status based on *what* an individual is externally. Support that champions the development of personal empowerment derived from *who* an individual is intrinsically and represents substantive character receives far less importance and relevance. This cleverly designed strategy influences an individual or group to participate in conceiving solutions and creating laws that nonsensically do nothing more than keep alive the chronic symptoms that immorally distress society.

There is an old adage that goes, "Repetition is an avenue to learning." Educate to the inherent qualities comprising substantive character, and the chronic symptoms that immorally plague society dissipate. They dissolve because hearts and minds are changed rather than simply seeking to alter behavior through developing theatrical and superfluous laws. The "more things change, the more they remain the same," as a vast number of individuals and groups, from the most powerful to the least powerful, continue to honor the pretense of credibility and relevance based on power, authority, and prominence. With this strategy, self-importance and self-indulgence motivated by self-will become primary motivators to procure credibility and relevance at any cost.

And if the behavior that represents evil is necessary to use in order to procure this goal, history has proven from humanity's beginning this is no problem to discharge. Remember, the intent of evil is to discredit and/or destroy human life along with its dignity. As necessary agents to help secure such gains, power, domination, and superiority must be exerted over other people to preserve external status and material possessions.

A reminder of this fact is articulated quite well by Dr. Linda M. Woolf, a professor of psychology and international human rights at Webster University. Dr. Woolf states:

> Mass violence, torture, violations of fundamental human rights, and the mistreatment of human beings is not a new aspect of humanity; documentation of such events spans the historical record. It is imperative that a greater understanding of the psychological, cultural, political, and societal roots of human cruelty, mass violence, and genocide be developed. We need to continue to examine the factors which enable individuals collectively and individually to perpetrate evil/genocide and the impact of apathetic bystanders as fuel for human violence. While an exact predictive model for mass violence/human cruelty is beyond

the scope of human capability, we have an obligation to develop a model that highlights the warning signs and predisposing factors for human violence and genocide. With such information, we can develop policies, strategies, and programs designed to counteract these atrocities.[12]

Any system of living that solely equates credibility and relevance with power, authority, prominence, and material possessions cultivates "the psychological, cultural, political, and societal roots of human cruelty, mass violence, and genocide."[13] When personal attributes such as innate intelligence, kindness, trust, ingenuity, reciprocity, and cooperation are deemed irrelevant, a model that highlights the warning signs and predisposing factors for human violence and genocide will have presented itself. The allegories of Inanna and Dumuzi and Adam and Eve reveal what has been a reality for humanity since its earliest history with respect to the lack of societal support for character development as soon as an individual enters this life.

Character development, which comprises a person's inherent credibility made manifest, is the prophylactic every individual is entitled to possess. This preventive agent protects against "the psychological, cultural, political, and societal roots of human cruelty, mass violence, and genocide"[14] from developing internally. And both allegories also reveal the training humanity has been exposed to throughout the ages to develop feelings of fear, shame, and embarrassment for qualities such as authenticity and vulnerability.

---

[12] Linda M. Woolf, PhD, "Holocaust, Genocide, and Human Rights," *Webster.edu*, http://faculty.webster.edu/woolflm/holocaust.html.

[13] Aisa Purak, "Rape as an Act of Genocide in Bosnia and Herzegovina from 1992–1995," (Graduate Thesis, Niagara University), 17.

[14] Purak, "Rape," 17.

The insight this allegory discloses is staggering concerning the willful adherence to exert self-will to achieve legitimacy, which only creates conditions ripe for relationship struggles involving power, domination, and superiority. Economic, racial, ethnic, gender, religious, and other disparities are naturally occurring symptoms when self-indulgence and self-importance are the masterminds behind establishing personal legitimacy. Again, when attaining external status and material possessions determine credibility and relevance, the end game is to attain power, domination, and superiority over other individuals. Adam and Eve choose to exercise their self-will rather than nurture the qualities comprising their inherent credibility that would develop their individual empowerment. And playing an extremely significant role in the allegory is the manipulative serpent reminiscent of a system of living cunningly offering advice and support for taking on a personal philosophy and psychology that represented perversion.

The tireless effort by cultural, political, religious, and societal "serpents" to nullify the importance of educating an individual to identify and value qualities representatives of inherent credibility has been a measured strategy. Absent throughout human history is a system of living that encourages a person to learn how they are defined by more than experiences due to embracing personal empowerment that represents authentic credibility and relevance. Of course not, because this form of education would be a definite threat to the malicious "serpents" who only serve the decree to attain positions of power, domination, and superiority. This decree divides people rather than uniting souls under a banner of community made possible from the intellectual, psychological, emotional, and spiritual wealth provided by the gift that keeps giving—inherent credibility.

As James Baldwin clearly states in his book, *No Name In The Street*:

> For power truly to feel menaced, it must somehow sense itself in the presence of another power—or, more accurately, energy—which it has not known how to control. Force does not work the way its advocates seem to think it does. It does not, for example, reveal to the victim the strength of his adversary. On the contrary, it reveals the weakness, even the panic of his adversary, and this revelation invests the victim with patience. Furthermore, it is ultimately fatal to create too many victims. The victor can do nothing with these victims, for they do not belong to him but to the victims.

They belong to the people he is fighting. The people know this, and as inexorably as the roll call—the honor roll—of victims expands, so does their will become inexorable: they resolve that these dead, their brethren, shall not have died in vain. When this point is reached, however long the battle may go on, the victor can never be the victor: on the contrary, all his energies, his entire life, are bound up in a terror he cannot articulate, a mystery he cannot read, a battle he cannot win—he has simply become the prisoner of the people he thought to cow, chain, or murder into submission.[15]

It is apparent systems that strictly recognize external status and material possessions as the sole means to establish legitimacy have been protected and upheld throughout humanity's history. It is also apparent throughout history that individuals and groups that have

---

[15] James Baldwin, *No Name in the Street* (New York: The Dial Press, 1972), 88–89.

attained economic, social, and religious dominance over others from this limited form of legitimacy are principal guardians of this system. Running a close second are the Inanna, Dumuzi, Adam and Eve protégés who are easily persuaded to abandon inherent credibility for the false equivalence of personal legitimacy. Both factions invest heavily in self-interest and have no genuine concern about the economic, social, and religious interests of other people. Pursuing "fool's gold" while sacrificing moral and character development is nothing more than self-indulgence personified.

But neither faction has historically demonstrated the ability to avoid succumbing to Baldwin's statement: "all his energies, his entire life, are bound up in a terror he cannot articulate, a mystery he cannot read, a battle he cannot win—he has simply become the prisoner of the people he thought to cow, chain, or murder into submission."[16] A long-established custom to supposedly manage the internal terror that has been adopted by the powerful, dominant, and purported superior has been to tighten the screws of discrimination and injustice. Violence against women, limited voting privileges, incarceration of Black and Brown, wage inequities, stricter healthcare, sophisticated bias due to gender, sexual orientation, race, ethnicity, age, the death penalty, and substandard public-school education are increased.

It is for this reason that more power, domination, and superiority over others have to be sustained to ward off the internal terror of feeling threatened with terms such as inherent credibility, personal empowerment, and impoverishment. The erroneous guidelines promoted by this system have consistently been designed to restrict personal value to the boundaries of external and material factors. Such misleading guidelines severely undervalue a person's all-inclusive worth. It is understandable that pursuing power, domination, and

---

[16] Baldwin, *No Name*, 89.

superiority over others becomes a person's primary goal in their life when they have been taught to fear their own shadow, which represents a worthy silhouette of individuality.

Genuine legitimacy and security encompass a person's unique and distinctive qualities of originality. Nonetheless, shortly after birth, culture and society combine to collaborate on training an individual to develop a dependency on external status and material assets rather than inherent credibility. With the exclusion of a person's inherent credibility that is based on attributes of meritorious character to reveal a more comprehensive personal value, the agenda of this system of living becomes quite clear. The goal is to pit one class, one race, one ethnicity, one gender, one religion, and the educated against one another.

Because inherent credibility is not used by this system to establish personal value, a methodical manipulation takes advantage of this absence. This deficiency motivates a person to internalize the belief that there is only one option available to develop their self-perception. Personal experiences are the only option to define oneself; good, bad, or indifferent. Lacking the knowledge and value attributed to inherent credibility restricts the ability of an individual to know that they are more than experiences. To further exaggerate the manipulation, if an individual's experiences are predominately positive, then self-perception is inflated.

And when an individual's experiences are predominately negative, self-perception is deflated. Distractive symptoms will dominate society due to this system of living equating personal value with external status and material possessions. Thus, when personal value is limited to being defined primarily by external and material factors, it is not uncommon for civility and moral development to morph into roadside casualties. When there is a deficiency regarding civil and moral development, the escalating loss of human life will be witnessed on a daily basis.

What can also be observed is a perpetual drive by the impoverished to create diminishing returns regarding a person's credibility and relevance. Day after day, mass killings of children and adults, hate crimes, gang violence, homelessness, alcoholism, drug addiction, appalling levels of poverty, suicide, depression, and other criminal activities provide the context to witness the diminishing returns. When an individual's value is primarily derived from sources other than one's inherent credibility and relevance, personal perversion begins the process of diminishing returns. The pursuit of power, domination, and superiority to possess any and all external sources is revealed as an individual becomes uncaringly driven to satisfy self-indulgence and self-interest at the expense of defiling another person or group's dignity. What emerges from this form of emotional, intellectual, and spiritual impoverishment are the economic, social, racial, and ethnic disparities that replace genuine credibility, relevance, and morality.

Victor Hugo in *Les Misérables* was correct when he stated:

> Teach the ignorant as much as you can; society is culpable in not providing a free education for all, and it must answer for the night which it produces. If the soul is left in darkness, sins will be committed. The guilty one is not he (or she) who commits the sin, but he (or she) who causes the darkness.[17]

Victor Hugo had the right idea in mind to educate the "ignorant" (the unaware) to recognize, value, and practice the best personal attributes an individual enters this life inherently possessing. However, the problem standing in the way of Hugo's recommendation is the

---

[17] Victor Hugo, *Les Misérables* (New York: Penguin Group, 2015), 16.

fact that humanity, from the beginning of its existence, is thousands of years down the road of ignoring this education. To starve the soul and invalidate personal empowerment in favor of attaining power, authority, and prominence groomed humanity to internalize self-betrayal and execute acts of betrayal with respect to relationships. Humanity's refusal to establish this educational curriculum has exiled "the collective soul to darkness" and inaugurated the long-standing pattern of chasing symptoms to solve this darkness.

The educational curriculum Victor Hugo speaks of will have to be actualized on a personal basis because the established power, authority, and prominent advocates will stop at nothing to kill a populace decree. This is to be expected, which has nothing to do with the personal effort that reads:

When I was young and naive, I wanted to change the world to be more open-minded and receptive to the needs of others considered different. Rather than champion levels of division, thrive to exemplify coalitions of equals. Lastly, broaden credibility, relevance, and value to include qualities that characterize intrinsic value. However, as I have aged and become less naive, I have come to realize that I am not that powerful and vain to change a world that is beyond my control. The best that I can do is change how I am in this domain by developing my own personal empowerment. And with this Herculean effort, I have indeed changed the world.

To reject and turn away from this Herculean effort helps to facilitate America remaining a victim of its own creations. Architect of the crippling moral effects of gender, class, racial, ethnic, religious, and social oppressions that have historically divided its populace. The internalized preoccupation with self-betrayal, and subsequent external acts of betrayal, will continue to be fueled by a condition of impoverishment: ignorance of one's inherent legitimacy. Relationships, in particular marriages and families, will be hard-pressed to remain intact because the impoverished define credibility, relevance, and value based on a hierarchical positioning of power, authority, and prominence. At the top of the relationship structure is the dominant figure expecting accommodation from the less dominant to sustain credibility, relevance, and value. Again, Victor Hugo had the right idea: feed the soul and validate personal empowerment that will establish within the relationship a coalition of equals.

Chapter 3

IRONY AND TRAGEDY

*Cowards rule the world today with
coward rules and coward customs.
To succeed, all you got to know is how
to blame and how to complain.
I truly believe it's the survival of the unfittest these days.*
—Yellowstone, Season 5, Episode 5

*When we are no longer able to change a situation,
we are challenged to change ourselves.*
—Viktor Frankl

As long as the recognition of economic, social, religious, political, racial, and ethnic prominence is deemed to be of greater value and relevance than inherent credibility associated with human life, the after-effect is predictable. Intellectual, emotional, and spiritual impoverishment prevails as a leading contributor to much of the populace's hypocritical relationship with morality. Lacking personal knowledge pertaining to innate credible attributes that represent an individual's core value leaves a person with only one option to define oneself. Self-perception is developed based on negative or positive experiences when living within a system that deems *what* an individual is externally of greater value than *who* an individual is intrinsically.

It is disingenuous to proclaim a fabricated concern and imaginary moral highroad toward the disadvantaged. The repercussion can be anticipated for both the disadvantaged and privileged as a result of being trained within a system of living married to defining credibility and relevance based on external success. Unaware of admirable intrinsic traits as legitimate qualifiers that determine personal value makes it easy for the disadvantaged to obediently identify themselves as unworthy, unlovable, or undeserving due to mounting negative experiences. Deceit arising from the privileged becomes intensified when affirmative self-perceptions are developed due to positive experiences. Within this system of living, positive experiences for the privileged mainly occur from advantages established due to the exertion of power, authority, and prominence over other individuals and groups for economic, social, religious, political, racial, and ethnic superiority. Hence, the presence of oppressive symptoms that represent impoverishment—such as injustice, discrimination, inequality, inequity, and incarceration—helps secure a position of superiority. It is not surprising to learn one fundamental function of charitable organizations is to accommodate the guilty conscious.

Vast numbers of the populace representing different factions have expressed their disapproval of the term impoverishment when used to explain the basic cause for society's massive failure to take reasonable care of human life. The list of failures is extensive: gun violence associated with the indiscriminate killing of children and adults; reproductive rights for countless numbers of women in the US dramatically restricted or denied; January 6, 2021, United States Capitol attack by more than 2000 rioters to overturn the 2020 Democratic election results; the nonexistence of a functioning and affordable healthcare system for millions of Americans; tuition costs continuing to increase as $1.75 trillion federal and private student debt loans remain outstanding; contentious and inflexible disputes between Democratic and Republican political parties pertaining to voting rights and restrictions that impact the BIPOC populace.[18]

Other failures to take reasonable care of human life include income inequality, unaffordable housing, domestic violence, indignant political disputes over what to do with legal and illegal immigrants, violent and verbal attacks directed at the LGBTQ community, mental health issues, alcohol and drug addictions, and the banning of books that contain sexual content, sexual assault, abortion, LGBTQ themes, race, and racism.[19] With respect to banning books with sexual content, this can be considered a violation of the freedom of speech and freedom of expression. Both freedoms are important rights that protect human dignity and life. Access to information, including books, is crucial for individuals to make informed choices and decisions about their lives. By limiting access to information and perspectives, banning books with sexual content could restrict individuals' ability to understand and navigate important aspects of their lives, such as sexuality and relationships. There is a strong argument to be made that banning books with sexual content constitutes a failure to take care of human life, as it can restrict access to information and perpetuate harmful societal attitudes and beliefs.

What energizes disapproval for the term impoverishment is the fact that many individuals within the populace have managed to

---

[18] Emmaline Soken-Huberty, "10 Examples of Social Issues in the US," *Human Rights Careers*, https://www.humanrightscareers.com/issues/examples-of-social-issues-in-the-us/

[19] Ella Feldman, "Over 1600 Books Were Banned During the Past School Year," *Smithsonian Magazine*, September 23, 2022, https://www.smithsonianmag.com/smart-news/whos-behind-the-push-to-ban-books-in-schools-180980818/.

achieve degrees of credibility and relevance linked to an external source. The source can be an economic or social status, occupation, race, ethnicity, or political or religious affiliations. What develops as a destructive attachment to an external source is the dependency that is established due to the quickly attained power, authority, and prominence. Developing a compulsory reliance on an external source is easy and trouble-free because it represents the only means available for an individual to experience credibility, relevance, and value. Compliance is the only prerequisite, and passivity is easy to come by for external sources when its validation is historically passed down as the only game in town. Pursuing external sources for legitimacy is then perceived as the lone pathway to experiencing power, authority, and prominence. This is an expected way of thinking for any individual unfamiliar with personal empowerment revealed through attributes comprising inherent credibility.

Though the example of achieving a populace consensus is less than desirable, for the only time in recorded history, humanity demonstrates a united front with respect to using the same model to achieve legitimacy. This collective effort temporarily allows adversarial demographics to rise above deeply rooted disputes pertaining to economic, gender, racial, ethnic, religious, and social inequalities. However, it should be noted that when a demographic decides to magnify its power, authority, and prominence by lessening the legitimacy of another demographic, impoverishment will always be the contributing instigator. This term refers to the intellectual, emotional, and spiritual deprivation an individual experiences as a result of lacking an awareness of admirable qualities that translate into inherent credibility, which is the basis for personal empowerment.

Even though there is antagonism between various factions of the populace, there is complete unity regarding their irritation with the term impoverishment. Class, gender, race, ethnicity, religion, employment, age, and access to quality of education differences have historically been consumed with hostilities. However, the harsh judgment toward the term impoverishment is maintained by the collective, even as this populace experiences a consistent and persistent display of moral depravity throughout the nation and global community on a daily basis. As a consequence of this historically based denial, the negative manifestation of impoverishment continues to provoke various factions within the human province to accept a perverted appetite for devouring its own kind. The prophetic words of the former Emperor of Ethiopia, Haile Selassie, cannot be overlooked: "Throughout history, it has been the inaction of those who could have acted; the indifference of those who should have known better; the silence of the voice of justice when it mattered most; that has made it possible for evil to triumph."[20]

Two self-inflicted wounds explain the reason various factions of humanity need to maintain their disapproval of the term impoverishment. Holding on to disapproval in the face of depravity that has absolutely no regard for the sanctity of human life is abominable. The disapproval rises to become repugnant with intensity because these same factions simultaneously are willing to commit violations against moral and principled standards. It is important to understand that hate crimes, discrimination, and injustice based on gender, racial, ethnic, religious, age, economic, and educational differences are symptoms of a deeper wound: impoverishment. The first wound has to do with a negative perception linked to impoverishment, which traditionally has been reserved for a specific segment of the populace. For decades the term has been attached to the poverty-stricken, homeless, poor, chronically unemployed, uneducated, habitual

---

[20] Emperor Haile Selassie, from an address in Addis Ababa, 1963.

criminal, and those addicted to drugs and alcohol. This characterization by numerous factions to portray these individuals as destitute and a willingness to live out this way of life has nothing to do with economics. On the contrary, this personal disposition has more to do with an internalized sense of poverty.

When there is a failure to attain external sources for validation within a system of living that equates this achievement with legitimacy, a person is left with one option to develop self-perception. A human tragedy closely linked to this system is that positive or negative experiences become the one available option to develop self-perception. With no other internal information to summon that would offset or negate the negative impact resulting from an inability to achieve credibility and relevance, a demoralized self-perception is cultivated. Examples of an inability to achieve or maintain credibility and relevance within this system of living are the breakup of a marriage or romantic relationship; the loss of a parent or child; the loss of a job or career; losing one's home or primary residence due to health issues or insufficient finances; or an inferior education.

What can become a precedent for an individual is to establish a way of life that is linked to a generational permanency of destitution. The internal transformation to one of being an indigent can be internalized effortlessly with the reinforcement of an overall approval of this process by the populace, which gathers intensity by its need to feel externally and materially superior to others. The moral and ethical neglect to educate a person to know they inherently possess qualities of merit that provide the opportunity to know they are more than just an accumulation of experiences is blatant. Solidifying this conspicuous omission are the practices of discrimination, injustice, and hatred. There is an outrageous willingness on the part of one segment of the populace—who has achieved credibility and relevance to commit violations against moral and principled standards—to remind another segment of their destitute and second-class standing. Again, the origin of this form of impoverishment on both sides of the scale goes far beyond the importance bestowed upon external importance and material resources.

The second self-inflicted wound that upholds censorship regarding the term impoverishment by different factions has to do with an egotistical need to develop a positive self-perception. With respect to gender, inter-gender, racial, interracial, religious, inter-religious, and so forth, presenting a positive self-perception even at the expense of denigrating another person or group is considered appropriate. Having achieved varying degrees of an unsavory legitimacy affords the victorious faction the opportunity to develop a personal view of themselves as being successful. Why? Because power, superiority, and authority over others have been achieved within a system that thrives on this agenda. The success achieved is a result of attaining legitimacy within a system of living that strictly equates credibility with external importance and material value. Exploitation, deceit, domination, and corruption used to attain this success are common practices. The attainment of credibility and relevance resulting from the practices of discrimination, inequity, and inequality is viewed as simply a cost of doing business.

When the prosperous are asked to appraise the degree of legitimacy concerning success achieved as a result of one or more inequitable practices being the difference—economic, gender, racial, ethnic, educational, or religious—a common response is, "I did not create the imbalance, nor was I around when the practices of discrimination, inequity, and inequality originated." Within this system of living, economic, social, religious, and political success is frequently achieved through the deliberate act of denying another person or group an equivalent opportunity to achieve success. The existence of practices culminating in discrimination, injustice, bigotry, and disproportioned incarceration helps to safeguard success for one person or group over another. For example, it does not matter if the economic system is capitalist, socialist, or communist—exploitation, deceit, and corruption will dominate because power, authority, and prominence are the goals to be achieved.

Acknowledgment of this primary motivation—to take advantage of a system of living that promotes an imbalanced economic, gender, racial, ethnic, educational, and religious way of life—as an internal state of impoverishment will never, ever be openly conceded. The tight-lipped confession that any degree of impoverishment exists helps to facilitate an external confidence and privilege that acts as a vanguard to distract from the actual truth. When the question is frequently asked toward the end of a conversation with a person experiencing this level of denial, the response is often: "Can another word be used instead of impoverishment?"

Again, the term impoverishment is purposely meant to include three distinct components of human life: intellectual, emotional, and spiritual. Evil and its tributaries, such as injustice, discrimination, jealousy, deceit, and betrayal, make their appearances through impoverishment. It is common for these damaging elements to emerge within human relationships when this type of impoverishment is left masked and not reformed for any length of time. Historically speaking, evil and its tributaries have heartlessly overshadowed relationships while conceiving the horrific loss of human life due to their wickedness. The dreadful reality is that evil remains extremely lethal because impoverishment has yet to be engaged with its deadly antagonist. Impoverishment's distinct adversary that would effectively diminish its influence is a dedicated social curriculum that would educate a person to recognize, value, and practice their inherent credibility.

The American essayist, poet, and philosopher Henry David Thoreau provided valuable insight when he stated: "That virtue we appreciate is as much ours as another's. We see so much as we possess."[21] It is exceedingly difficult for a person to see what they innately possess if humanity, as a whole, continues to exclude inherent credibility from a committed program of study with its focus on the development of virtues such as authenticity, legitimacy, and community. Absent this education allows an exhausted and haggard melodrama to persevere. Many factions within the human domain will continue to be influenced by a collective apathy to accept the perverted appetite to devour its own kind. Indifference inevitably is to vanish in order to extend a lifeline to humankind that circumvents its self-inflicted demise. And the lifeline is inherent credibility personified through a substantive character that will effectively lessen the attraction to this perverted appetite.

Conversely, the unwillingness to integrate educational training that teaches an individual to identify and practice the best attributes they possess in this life only perpetuates dire consequences. In the Paramount Network television drama series *Yellowstone*, the character John (played by Kevin Costner) states: "I've come to think perfection only lives in little moments. Can't be sustained over hours, just instances. Little wisps of time and the world becomes imperfect again."[22] It is common behavior to flaunt the appearance of perfection within a system of living that attaches greater value based on *what* an individual is externally than *who* an individual is intrinsically.

---

[21] Henry David Thoreau, *Thoreau's Journals* (UK: Delphi Classics, 2017).

[22] *Yellowstone*, Season 5, Episode 6, "Cigarettes, Whiskey, a Meadow and You," directed by Taylor Sheridan, aired December 11, 2022, on Paramount Network, https://www.paramountnetwork.com/shows/yellowstone.

Kevin Costner's character John is exactly correct. Within a system of living devoid of a social curriculum that trains an individual to recognize, value, and practice the best inherent qualities a person can inherently possess, perfection becomes little whisps of time before returning to a state of impoverishment. Education toward character development unveils meritorious attributes that allow an individual to be accountable when mistakes do occur. To be good and to do good involves being responsible, reliable, and expressing humility. Character development paves the way to being a good person rather than pursuing a facade of perfection, which is a crude technique to conceal intellectual, emotional, and spiritual impoverishment.

Up to this point in history, humanity's moral development has been terribly limited to merely verbalizing words that are nothing more than ethical nuances. The honorable qualities a person innately possesses have been designated as immaterial in relation to external prominence and material resources. Yet again, this neglect breeds intellectual, emotional, and spiritual deficits that subsequently encourage injustice, deceit, and betrayal to dominate relationships. It is evident the problem that factions of society have with accepting a condition of internal impoverishment while living in the midst of material affluence, external prominence, power, and superiority.

Throughout the ages, factions of people have established a custom that solidifies their credibility and relevance exclusively based on external status and material assets. As limiting and awkward as this legitimacy may appear on the surface, all the same, it has served to provide refuge, solace, and security for the various groups. Just as important, this form of legitimacy has also provided meaning and purpose. This would include financial notoriety, race, ethnicity, gender, career, social prominence, religion, and/or political affiliations. Once a personal investment has taken place with respect to surrendering individuality and autonomy to the external source pursued to achieve legitimacy, what ensues is written in stone. This rigid stance of certitude will not be supplanted by an outside source. Any attempt to take away or nullify this sacrifice by a different faction will be met with intense resistance that includes a willingness to die for the sacrifice. The passing of laws and regulations to insert balance among the different groups is simply pointless. Rather than focusing on changing impoverished-motivated behavior, elevating the hearts and minds of people and a genuine sense of community stands to emerge.

There are varying definitions of tribalism. According to Dictionary.com, tribalism is defined as "behavior and attitudes that stem from strong loyalty to one's own tribe or social group."[23] This steadfast loyalty that is reinforced with behavior and attitudes should not be considered casual gestures. When a collection of individuals are principally in need of group identity to derive personal meaning and purpose, one decisive result is foreseeable—a multidimensional strategy that encourages another tribe or other groups to experience an equivalent legitimacy across the human spectrum will not be allowed to be established. Income, gender, racial, ethnic, voting rights, educational, and healthcare equality will be strongly opposed.

Again, personal value, meaning, and purpose within a system of living that bases credibility and relevance on *what* an individual is regarding social standing and material resources has a reward that involves the attainment of power, superiority, and authority. With this system, it becomes a day-to-day occurrence that different tribes contest with one another, as well as within the group, for these critical rewards. How can humanity be expected to do otherwise than to

---

[23] *Dictionary.com*, "tribalism (*n.*)," accessed January 27, 2023, https://www.dictionary.com/browse/tribalism.

inhibit or destroy one another when lacking any training concerning inherent credibility and relevance as a pathway to develop honorable character?

The Sudan Tribune adds to the discussion regarding tribalism:

> Tribalism implies the possession of a strong cultural or ethnic identity that separates one member of a group from the members of another group. Based on strong relations of proximity and kinship, as well as relations based on the mutual survival of both the individual members of the tribe and for the tribe itself, members of a tribe tend to possess a strong feeling of identity. The word 'tribe' can be defined to mean an extended kin group or clan with a common ancestor or can also be described as a group who shares the common interest of mutual survival and preservation of a common culture. The proverb "birds of a feather flock together" describes homophily, the human tendency to form friendship networks with people of similar occupations, interests, and habits.

These negative aspects of tribalism are often fueled by competition and the perception of a common threat. They promote fear, anxiety, and prejudice, all of which make us more susceptible to fake news, propaganda, and conflict. Tribalism can take many forms in our modern society. Loyalty to a tribe or other social group especially when combined with strong negative feelings for people outside the group. Tribalism within the group is strong. With a negative connotation and in a political context, tribalism can also mean discriminatory behavior or attitudes toward out-groups, based on in-group loyalty.[24]

---

[24] Peter Gai Manyuon, "Tribalism and Violence in South Sudan," *The Sudan Tribune*, February 6, 2014, accessed February 8, 2023, https://sudantribune.com/article48750/.

Without question, a person can be associated with a tribe and not participate in tribalism. For example, gender, race, ethnicity, and nationality link an individual to a specific tribe. Even though the association exists, a person can decide not to use the group as a primary source for defining personal value, status, and importance. Sustaining this autonomy requires training to identify and develop personal attributes of substantive character that provide authentic value, meaning and purpose beyond the cosmetic tribal or group identifications.

Various classes, races, ethnicities, religions, age groups, pro-choice, pro-life, Democrat, Republican, professional, athlete, and the military all qualify as tribes that are used by different individuals to define their personal value, meaning, and purpose. The need to attach one's identity and to experience value, meaning, and purpose from an external source is exclusively motivated by an internal condition of impoverishment. What accompanies this impoverishment and is easily detected is an individual's obsession with flaunting their self-importance and self-indulgence while minimizing the credibility and relevance of another person or group. Power, superiority, and authority are badges of honor sought after by this person who takes advantage of disparity within a system limiting credibility and relevance to external prominence and material resources.

Tribes are a natural outgrowth across a diverse human spectrum. Tribalism is a natural outgrowth of groups living within a system that is deficient in educating each tribe to embrace personal empowerment that would encourage the creation of a coalition of equals. This insightful training would include the recognition and development of innate qualities that represent an ethical and moral character. Another benefit arising from this undertaking is the opportunity an individual has to develop personal meaning and purpose beyond just a tribal or group identification. Emerging as a consequence of this deficiency is the ability for tribalism to thrive as a one-dimensional protective mindset unique to the explicit particulars of the faction. Remaining loyal to this one-dimensional mindset eventually exposes a predictable and expected outcome. As stated, any attempt to initiate a multidimensional way of life with an intent to achieve legitimacy for a different class, gender, race, ethnicity, religion, political party, gang, or different social distinction is deemed unacceptable. For any tribe, a threat to self-importance and self-indulgence that will undercut a previously established power, superiority, and authority will be met with great resistance.

The push for a coalition of equals among the various tribes endangers existing income, gender, racial, ethnic, religious, and social imbalances. As just stated, this move toward a real sense of community is considered as having no chance of succeeding or being effective within a system of living that thrives on inequities and inequalities. Historically speaking, groups seeking to elevate credibility and relevance to equal tribes in positions of power, authority, and prominence simply do not occur. The prudent words of the Irish poet and playwright Oscar Wilde come to mind when the price is known for willfully disregarding individuality and autonomy: "Nowadays people know the price of everything and the value of nothing."[25] It is difficult to grasp the immeasurable value of autonomy and individuality when a person is willing to follow with blind obedience merciless standards of oppression that dehumanize, rather than enhance, human life.

However comforting and assuring tribalism may appear on the surface, significant information on a personal basis is revealed beneath

---

[25] Oscar Wilde, *The Picture of Dorian Gray* (Germany: Bernhard Tauchnitz,1908), 64.

the surface. Behind this facade of comfort and safety is a state of intellectual, emotional, and spiritual impoverishment. Life for various groups of people satisfied with living this facade of comfort requires constant personal reinforcement pertaining to their self-importance and self-indulgence. The reinforcement helps to maintain this unstable way of life. The requirement to establish a relationship with a person or persons subscribing to this way of life is to appease their self-importance and self-indulgence. Bloviation emphasizing economic, social, racial, ethnic, political, and religious status massages the fragile ego. Whereas a multidimensional approach favors inclusion, diversity, and community that translates into a gathering of coalitions rather than pacifying the impulse for empire-building. The one-dimensional strategy consistently reveals an ill-conceived commitment to fulfill self-interest, no matter its failure to integrate integrity and uphold morality throughout the process.

In review, the notion of empire-building is a plan of action chiefly motivated by impoverishment, which reveals an absence of moral and ethical development. It is not uncommon for nations, communities, and families to become bitterly divided and fragmented due to adherence to a one-dimensional strategy. This tactic is energized by an incentive to attain power, superiority, and authority along the lines of economic, racial, ethnic, gender, religious, and social disparities. It is a frequent practice within a system that equates power, superiority, and authority with legitimacy to take advantage of a populace that can easily be distracted by inflated importance ascribed to tribalism.

The value of educating an individual to recognize their inherent credibility and relevance— comprised of the best qualities that a person brings into their life—ensures the development of moral and ethical character. To be linked with a specific tribe or group can be a worthy union. Developing moral and ethical character acts as a safeguard against surrendering autonomy and individuality to an external source. Establishing credibility and relevance in shallow conditions is eliminated as a viable possibility. Just as important, this safeguard secures personal freedom. Educating a populace to recognize their inherent credibility and relevance that represent qualities of excellence permits nations, societies, and families to effectively live amongst one another with differences but in harmony.

The will to live an authentic existence is a derivative of this ethical development. Lacking this derivative dictates an evolution of social injustices and disparities. Throughout the ages, to keep the will-to-survive mentality alive, which is in direct opposition to the will-to-live, the value of human life had to be diminished harshly. Humanity has engaged in genocide; ethnic cleansing; unjust internment; enslavement; torture; rape and sexual violence; political repression; racial, ethnic, gender, and age discrimination; religious persecution; suicide bombing; state terrorism or state-sponsored terrorism; beheadings and lynching; murder and massacres; death squads; unethical human experimentation; gang warfare; kidnappings and forced disappearances. Throughout the global community, the sadistic use of power, supremacy, and authority has expressed its vice-like grip with impoverishment due to humanity's inability to establish a determined conviction toward the development of personal autonomy and individuality.

The words of James Baldwin, an American novelist, essayist, poet, and activist, fittingly apply to whether this issue of impoverishment—in existence since the birth of humankind—can be diminished or eliminated. Baldwin states: "Not everything that is faced can be changed, but nothing can be changed until it is faced."[26] And

---

[26] James Baldwin, "As Much Truth as One Can Bear," *New York Times Book Review* (January 14, 1962), Section T, Page 11.

the legendary American novelist, literary critic, and scholar Ralph Ellison adds: "Life is to be lived, not controlled; and humanity is won by continuing to play in the face of certain defeat."[27] A system of living over three thousand years old that dismisses inherent credibility as an irrefutable legitimacy equivalent to transitory forms of external legitimacy may never change. However, there could be a possibility of change to occur by continuing to draw attention to how the lack of moral judgment reveals a condition of impoverishment. This form of impoverishment drastically influences an individual to deliberately undermine either form of credibility and relevance pertaining to another person or group of people. The American writer, philosopher, and political activist Susan Sontag had it right when she stated: "I want to make a New Year's prayer, not a resolution. I'm praying for courage."[28]

[27] Ralph Ellison, *Invisible Man* (New York: Penguin, 1952), 465.

[28] Susan Sontag, *As Consciousness Is Harnessed to Flesh: Journals and Notebooks 1964–1980* (New York: Farrar Straus Giroux, 2012), 322.

Chapter 4

THE CONTINUED PURSUIT TO DISCREDIT

*Everything can be taken from a man
(woman) but one thing:
the last of human freedoms—
to choose one's attitude in any given set of circumstances,
to choose one's own way.
—Viktor Frankl*

*Life can only be understood backwards;
but it must be lived forwards.
—Soren Kierkegaard*

When credibility and relevance are not based on a person's inherent legitimacy, rejection by an external source can easily be internalized as a negative experience. It becomes effortless to define one's self-perception as not enough, unacceptable, and unlovable. This system makes it an impossibility to trust another person with one's aspirations, frailties, loyalty, triumphs, and affection when the end game is about the attainment of power, authority, and dominance. On a grander scale, this deficiency has greatly diminished the opportunity for women to disagree with one another and not demonize one another due to differences.

The lack of appreciation for qualities that represent substantive character has led women, as well as society, to be easily manipulated by a distorted and perverse masculinity. This distorted and perverted masculinity strictly pursues power, authority, and domination to use against women—and society as a whole. The mechanism used to accomplish this goal is evil, which has the intent to discredit and destroy. To trust the confession while enlisting signature attributes such as accountability, forgiveness, compassion, vigilance, and fortitude establishes the seeds of personal empowerment. The time has arrived to stop reacting to the antagonist, be it gender inequality, racism, classism, ageism, and discrimination against sexual orientation.

Aside from the nation's fierce and contentious spectacle of economic, political, racial, and social tensions, there is one controversial and notable social issue that has continually generated an intense populace debate for generations. The issue involves whether a woman has the right or not to make a reproductive decision together with medical consultation to terminate her pregnancy with an abortion. What has kept this issue so combative and unresolved for decades is the fact that it has been notoriously hijacked by tribalism. One-dimensional strategies with a sole focus that one side of the discussion exercise ultimate authority over the other side has dominated the debate throughout the years. Democratic and Republican political parties, pro-life and pro-choice enthusiasts, religious and secular factions, countless states within the Union, the degreed and non-degreed, and the judicial courts have participated in this winner-take-all mentality.

Unfortunately, the unpromising influence of impoverished thinking is evident from both sides of the reproductive discussion. There is a lack of compassion, empathy, support, and awareness regarding the repetitious attempt to legislate women into surrendering their autonomy and individuality. The age-old strategy of dividing women along the lines of morality is the psychology employed to achieve this form of oppression. NPR.org reported: "In a historic and far-reaching decision, the US Supreme Court's decision in Dobbs v. Jackson Women's Health Organization officially reversed *Roe v. Wade* on June 24, 2022, declaring that the constitutional right to abortion, upheld for nearly a half-century, no longer exists." To support the Supreme Court's decision, pro-life enthusiasts influenced the governments of Alabama, Arkansas, Idaho, Kentucky, Louisiana, Mississippi, Missouri, Oklahoma, North Dakota, South Dakota, Tennessee, Texas, West Virginia, and Wisconsin to ban abortions with no exception for rape or incest. Several states also banned abortions after a set amount of weeks: Georgia (6), Iowa (6), Nebraska (12), North Carolina (12), Arizona (15), Florida (15), and Utah (18).

After a state's designated weeks of pregnancy have passed, a woman and her medical provider are not entitled to make a reproductive decision that could terminate the pregnancy by having an abortion. The new abortion laws also specifically targeted medical providers who perform an abortion, as well as anyone who aids or intends to aid with abortion through civil lawsuits. It is of interest to note that enforcement of the Texas and Florida laws through civil lawsuits excludes litigation against the abortion patient. Just as interesting to note is how the Texas government has cleverly removed itself from enforcing the new abortion law and instead passed the enforcement responsibility onto private citizens.[29]

This type of thinking and problem-solving ignores a multidimensional solution that would allow for both sides of the issue to benefit. The multidimensional solution would necessitate both sides of the debate to compromise by lessening their positions on inflexible dimensions. The ability to compromise would allow each side to walk away from the conflict with a perception of victory. For example, pro-life

---

[29] Hughes, et al, "Senate Bill No. 8," https://capitol.texas.gov/tlodocs/87R/bill-text/pdf/SB00008H.pdf.

enthusiasts would renounce "with no exception for rape or incest" and settle for twelve weeks before terminating a pregnancy. Pro-choice enthusiasts would support the right of states to ban abortion after a twelve-week pregnancy, which would also include a woman and her medical provider not being entitled to make a reproductive decision after the pregnancy period.

The rewards of a multidimensional approach are threefold: overcoming the historically based attempt to completely oppress the autonomy and individuality of women, avoiding civil lawsuits against medical providers, and the overall reduction in abortions. Rather than take advantage of this multidimensional approach, tribalism continues to erode what could have been a *beautiful thing* to experience. In the words of the American poet and novelist Benjamin Alire Saenz, "To be careful with people and with words was a rare and beautiful thing."[30] The inability of enthusiasts on either side of the issue to be *careful with people and with words* has created a moral decay forestalling a reasonable outcome with respect to a woman's reproductive rights.

It is important to remember that tribalism thrives due to being established as a protective, one-dimensional strategy unique to the explicit particulars of the group. Impoverishment will regularly be revealed through one-dimensional strategies that exclude stratagems representing the credibility and relevance of other tribes or groups. The explicit particulars for the pro-life tribe involve becoming the self-appointed guardians of the unborn regardless of the cost to the mother if the statement "with no exception for rape or incest" is left to stand. The impoverished state governments insisting on this statement being an integral component of the ban on abortion have been successful in seductively enlisting an impoverished faction to engage in the act of oppression. Having citizen vigilantes carry out acts of oppression initiated by an

---

[30] Benjamin Alire Saenz, *Aristotle and Dante Discover the Secrets of the Universe* (New York: Simon & Schuster, 2012).

external source is the oldest con game that originated with the Adam and Eve allegory.

Before going any further with this discussion, it is important to highlight one critical concern involving the abortion debate. So long as the ban on abortion includes "with no exception for rape or incest" with respect to the expectant woman, it is meaningless for pro-choice enthusiasts to engage pro-life counterparts in the abortion debate. There is no question that there exist pro-life enthusiasts motivated by honorable moral beliefs. However, when the well-being of an expectant woman is not taken into consideration to determine whether she is a victim of rape or incest, the question arises: to what degree are moral beliefs compromised by the need to experience power, authority, and prominence? There is no question pro-life enthusiasts are correct: Widespread abortions can be social and moral issues that negatively impact this nation, as well as on an intercontinental basis. According to the World Health Organization, roughly 73 million induced abortions occur worldwide each year, with 61 percent of all unintended pregnancies and 29 percent of all pregnancies in general ending with an abortion. Russia, China, Cuba, Vietnam, Romania, and Bulgaria have historically struggled with high abortion rates for varying reasons.[31]

Conversely, infringing upon a woman's right to experience her autonomy, credibility, and relevance with respect to reproductive decisions does not and will not faithfully address the abortion issue in this nation. Teach women, men, and children to recognize, value, and practice their inherent credibility that represents substantive character, and one predictable result is certain. Pro-life supporters, pro-choice enthusiasts, and all of society will be morally elated to experience the reduction of abortions as a social and ethical malaise. Historically and contemporaneously speaking, the poor, young, undereducated, and vulnerable

---

[31] "Abortion Rates by Country," World Population Review, https://worldpopulationreview.com/country-rankings/abortion-rates-by-country

women have been victimized and susceptible to the power, abuse, and misuse of men. Until the education to substantive character becomes a moral staple within this system of living, the proclamation, "with no exception for rape or incest," regarding the lack of concern for the well-being of the expectant woman will continue to aid and abet the male perpetrator and victimization associated with the ban on abortion.

When debating whether twelve weeks versus six weeks is appropriate to determine pregnancy, rape, incest, or any other related condition, the abortion debate becomes even more problematic. Prior to the US Supreme Court's decision in Dobbs v. Jackson Women's Health Organization that officially reversed *Roe v. Wade*, Pro-choice enthusiasts "held out hope" that pro-life supporters would soften their stance regarding the six-week line of demarcation. The hope was qualities such as empathy, consideration, gallantry, and integrity would come into play and influence the thinking of pro-life enthusiasts to embrace a longer time period. However, when reaching the final stages of making public the new abortion laws, pro-life supporters fervently argued that six weeks was enough time to determine whether a woman was pregnant.

Without a reputable social curriculum to train a person to identify, value, and practice virtues of substantive character that cultivate the development of a moral blueprint, the obsession with one-dimensional thinking becomes inevitable. Within this system of living, because credibility and relevance are equated with the attainment of power, authority, and prominence, it is effortless to become fixated on employing manipulation, discrimination, and injustice to achieve legitimacy. The poor, young, undereducated, and vulnerable woman becomes a chessboard pawn sacrificed by power, authority, and prominence in order for a faction of the populace to achieve credibility and relevance. This theme can be witnessed throughout the history of humankind where white, Black, indigenous, People of Color, women, and the young are clashing with one another, including within the communities, through the use of power, authority, and prominence for credibility and relevance.

It is important to understand the consequences of how an unconstrained one-dimensional strategy can negatively impact a culture. This strategy is solely motivated by self-indulgence and self-importance to satisfy a fixation with acquiring power, superiority, and authority. As an after-effect of impoverishment, oppressive undertakings directed toward another person or group become a conceivable endeavor. The pro-life enthusiasts consisting of men and women give an appearance of being invested in exerting power, superiority, and authority over groups of women financially unable to have an abortion performed in the tranquil company of a discreet medical doctor. An obvious contradiction that is historically based is exposed with the states supporting new abortion laws. Women in a fiscal position to financially afford to have a tactful medical doctor perform a quiet abortion will continue to do. The ability to exercise self-government and individualism will remain unimpeded should they choose to have an abortion. The dignity and well-being of women representing this economic class are well protected due to an intellectual, emotional, and spiritual impoverishment revealed through practices of discrimination.

An effective method for impoverishment to indulge its obsession with power, authority, and prominence is to establish laws that silence the autonomy and individuality of women lacking external prominence and material resources. To persist in returning to an age-old strategy of gender and class discrimination to diminish a group of women's credibility and relevance also impacts their social legitimacy in a negative manner. A system of living that equates credibility and relevance with external status and material resources divides the populace against itself, with power, superiority, and authority being the end game. Again, the pro-life intentions to pursue this end game are revealed by a lack of empathy linked to the statement "with no exception for rape or incest." This will inevitably cause distress for women outside of economic and class distinction, who are once again being required to surrender their autonomy and individuality, which are significant sources to experience empowerment.

The acclaimed Morgan Simon, a freelance journalist, financial adviser, and activist, expressed her thoughts and concerns in a *Forbes Magazine* editorial on September 2, 2021. Simon states:

> Abortion is a contentious issue in America that has us just about perfectly divided, with 49 percent of people polling as pro-choice, 47 percent as anti-abortion in 2021. But whether you are fiercely pro-choice or fiercely supportive of banning abortion—you should be shocked and outraged by the undemocratic nature of this law, the way it turns neighbor against neighbor, and how it provides a bizarre economic incentive to do so.

> The law invites citizens to sue each other for a minimum of $10,000 if they suspect someone of "aiding and abetting" an abortion after the six-week cutoff. It sets a dangerous precedent for any number of social issues, by putting money not just into politics, but into actual policy.

> As Americans, it's ok for us to fight about our policy positions, but we should fight fair. Whether such a structure is applied to abortion, gun control, environmental regulations, or any number of contentious issues, it's highly problematic in its circumventing of

the Supreme Court, and its tying of dollar signs to the enforcement of a law. In their stated attempt to protect souls, advocates for this law are selling the soul of America.

As financially and socially astute as Morgan Simon has demonstrated to be throughout her life, there appear to be degrees of naïveté very much alive and well within her personal portfolio. Simon proclaims, "You should be shocked and outraged by the undemocratic nature of this law, the way it turns neighbor against neighbor, and how it provides a bizarre economic incentive to do so." In response to this statement, it is important to understand one critical reality. The new abortion laws enacted by Alabama, Arkansas, Idaho, Kentucky, Louisiana, Mississippi, Missouri, Oklahoma, North Dakota, South Dakota, Tennessee, Texas, West Virginia, Wisconsin, Georgia, Iowa, Nebraska, North Carolina, Arizona, Florida, and Utah are not meant to be democratic. They are meant to be exactly what they clearly ordain: power, superiority, and authority carried out through the distinct practices of class and gender discrimination. This entire strategy is in support of a repressive and one-dimensional strategy that diminishes the credibility and relevance of other people—in this instance, women.

Ms. Simon either refuses to acknowledge or fails to understand that the system of living she has consistently served establishes credibility and relevance solely based on an individual's external status and material resources. The more prominent an individual's status and resources, the more pronounced the power, superiority, and authority that person will assimilate. Therefore, this system of living is purposely designed to pit neighbor against neighbor, class against class, race against race, gender against gender, union against non-union, religion against religion, and youth against experience.

And if this discordant scheme is not thorough enough to create division, this system can intentionally pit members of the same class, gender, race, ethnicity, family, religion, and political affiliation against one another. This is all made possible because, within this system, legitimacy has nothing to do with virtues representing inherent credibility that can translate into substantive character. Instead, external prominence determines credibility and relevance, which, in turn, seduces an individual to develop personal goals that primarily involve the acquisition of power, superiority, and authority.

Ms. Simon also states, "It's ok for us to fight about our policy positions, but we should fight fair." The question emerges as to where Ms. Simon's economic and social perspectives were developed. The viewpoints she expresses come across as having been nurtured in a protective and sterile environment. Collectively speaking, history speaks for itself in revealing that many Americans have never been exposed to the type of training to identify, value, and practice the qualities that develop substantive character. To bitterly fight amongst one another in an unfair manner and oftentimes fight to the death over different policy positions is an enormous fraction of the American economic, political, racial, religious, and social histories. For many Americans, the need to be right takes precedence over the words of Anais Nin, the French-Cuban American diarist and essayist, when facing a stranger, colleague, or friend during an issue that creates conflict. She states: "Each friend represents a world in us, a world possibly not born until they arrive."[32]

Because there is a historical deficiency regarding this training as a society, deceit, contempt, and hatred are the tools most used to fight amongst one another. To fight fair with one another would

---

[32] Anais Nin, *The Diary of Anais Nin, Volume 1: 1931-1934* (Mariner Books, 1969).

necessitate establishing a socially based educational curriculum that teaches the legitimacy of qualities comprising inherent credibility. Under this scenario, a fair fight would be refereed under the watchful eye of character development to ensure that any infighting is reflective of ethical and principled behavior. The words of First Lady Eleanor Roosevelt came to mind when she said: "People grow through experience if they meet life honestly and courageously. That is how character is built."[33]

On September 9, 2021, another editorial appeared in the *Los Angeles Times*. This editorial was written by the *Times* editorial board titled: "To Stop the Texas Abortion Law, Congress Has to Act."

> The relentless onslaught finally paid off for states determined to roll back abortion rights. The Supreme Court, in a 5–4 decision, refused to block, even temporarily, an abominable Texas law that effectively disallows abortions when cardiac activity can be detected—starting at about six weeks of pregnancy, when most women don't even know they are pregnant—and empowers citizens to enforce it by suing anyone who helps a woman get an abortion. At the same time, legislators and governors in other states hostile to abortion rights, such as South Dakota, Florida, Arkansas, and South Carolina, have signaled their intention to consider laws similar to the Texas measure.

What is of interest regarding this editorial is located at the end of its title: "Congress Has to Act." The question arises as to what were the fundamental elements of this esteemed group of women

---

[33] Lorena A. Hickok, *Reluctant First Lady* (Creative Media Partners, 2017).

and men that influenced the *Times* editorial board to assert that "to stop the Texas abortion law, Congress has to act"? The naive observer of congressional affairs could assume three basic influences the board might have considered. At the time this editorial was written, the 117 Congress occupied the chambers. Senators and House of Representatives totaled approximately 538 members, and of this number, 147 were women. At first glance, the chance that Congress could effect a positive change regarding the "abominable Texas law," with congressional women amounting to 27 percent of the total membership, would appear to be one influence.

Another influence the board might have considered is of a religious nature. A majority of congressional members identify themselves as Christian and associated with a Protestant denomination. To protect women outside the ranks of economic and social distinctions from the act of repressing their autonomy and individuality may have been a consideration for the board. Elevating the congressional religious tribe to levels of the pious and dutiful to answer this call may have been a stretch but is still worth considering as an influence. The third consideration may have been an age factor. House of Representatives members averaged fifty-eight years of age, and senators averaged sixty-four years of age. Again, at first glance, the board could assume congressional members in their fifties and sixties would have developed in the latter stages of their lives a matured appreciation for attributes an individual inherently possesses, such as autonomy and individuality.

However, after careful reflection regarding past and current congressional relationships, further deliberation was suspended. The recollection of congressional relationships did not coincide with the above-stated considerations the *Times* editorial board may have thought existed. During the past three to four presidential administrations, extending over a quarter of a century, Congress has transformed itself into a collective expression of political dysfunction. Extreme partisanship and bitterness, as well as absolute opposition to the idea of compromise, characterize the nature of relationships throughout Congress as a whole.

When opposing viewpoints are at the center of a legislative agenda, rather than demonstrate an example of community for the populace to emulate in their relationships, models of antagonism and defiance are demonstrated. Tribalism becomes a common denominator the esteemed seek for refuge, with bitter division being another model for the populace to embrace. It does not matter that women have become an integral faction of the congressional membership. Whether inside the same political party or on opposite sides of the aisle, women do not converse on a polite basis with one another.

A similar dysfunction can be witnessed amongst members of the Christian faith with Protestant affiliations. Some of the pious and dutiful, in theory, unmask to serve self-interest and unabashedly deplore any perception that brotherhood or sisterhood may exist when different perspectives are being expressed. What takes precedence over principle is the badge of honor that conveys Democrat, Republican, Independent, Moderate, Progressive, Fiscal Conservative, Liberal, Dove, or Hawk. For this legislative body to respond with integrity, directness, and humility to the *Times* editorial board's petition that "Congress has to act" is a reach too far. To intervene and save a nondescript faction of women from an act of repression runs far too great of a risk to take when their own self-indulgence and self-importance could be placed in jeopardy due to standing against impoverishment. Congressional careers can come to a sudden end when power, superiority, and authority sense a perceived threat.

Forget about equating maturity with age when what is often revealed with older congressional members are juvenile tendencies with a fascination to attain and retain power, superiority, and authority.

Congress has proven time and time again an affinity to protect its own self-interest, which is to retain the esteemed status of either a senator or member of the House of Representatives. It is important to remember that the ultimate drive for one-dimensional thinking is to acquire more power and control at any cost. It is this limited cognitive function that permits emotional, intellectual, and spiritual impoverishment to prosper. Once more, when a system of living bases credibility and relevance predominantly on a person's external status and material resources, one-dimensional thinking is generated.

Self-importance and self-indulgence must be protected if one is to maintain power, authority, and domination, as this system of living rewards a person based on their external status and material resources. Together, impoverishment and one-dimensional thinking help sustain one another's existence. Favorable and unfavorable personal experiences become the lone options for developing self-perception. To apply experiences that will either inflate or deflate self-perception is to limit a person's view to external and material contexts. Absent from this equation are pertinent innate qualities that allow a person to separate themselves emotionally and intellectually from experiences. The lack of training to identify, value, and practice qualities of inherent credibility that represent substantive character permits an individual to develop a self-perception that is not polluted by positive, negative, or indifferent experiences.

For a vast number of women throughout the global community, becoming a mother remains a top priority. Generally speaking, being a mother is socially accepted as a significant component of experiencing womanhood. This is a reason the maternal experience remains a high-level ambition for many women. The recognizable identity as a mother is equivalent to the importance of its social acceptance. And just as significant to these two socially accepted roles is the lack of recognition with respect to their importance by a tribe of men and women representing economic prominence and social distinctions elitism. This is evidenced by their support for the repressive abortion laws in Texas, Florida, and Oklahoma, which will soon be enacted by other states under the banner of a pro-life agenda.

It is important to realize that cultural standards and practices, political agendas, and fiscal policies for society are, for the most part, determined by the individuals representative of this group. The reluctance by the elite to acknowledge the importance of a group of women not representative of economic prominence and social distinction has a great deal to do with the maternal involvement these women have historically played regarding humanity's process of evolution. The credibility and relevance achieved by this group are a threat to the elite because this recognition is attained outside of the power, superiority, and authority strategy. Historically, mothers have established an ironclad legitimacy for their contribution to humanity's ability to experience regeneration and resurgence.

In addition, women throughout the global community who live outside of economic prominence and social distinction have unambiguously stepped into the position as the primary custodian of the household. Responsibilities have included making certain the basic education, health concerns, and standard of living for the family as a whole are sustained. According to the Pew Research Center: "Women make up at least 40 percent of the workforce in more than eighty countries with data from 2010 to 2016. Across all of these countries, the median female share of the workforce is 45.4 percent." And during this current era, women outside the elite economic and social circles can be observed as upper and middle managers across a variety of industries.

The contributions made by these women involve primary business activities that include business, retail, education, government, clerical, technology, medical, military, agriculture, entertainment, and sports. The contributions have successfully met the needs of the current generation without compromising future generations. Nevertheless, these same women remain challenged to develop multidimensional strategies that support a continued appreciation and value attributed to autonomy, individuality, personal empowerment, and community.

The courage and resilience to triumph over persistent attempts by the economic and social elites to preserve a one-dimensional strategy that weakens a woman's ability to experience autonomy and individuality will be essential attributes needed for the present day and the future. With this as a commitment, the attributes will be too embedded in a spirit and soul that preempts policies of exclusion. At the same time, the opening to promote multidimensional strategies that consist of inclusion and equality will be present.

Wage inequality, oppressive religions, voting constraints, abortion restrictions, and violence committed against women will not overshadow the essence of human life when validated through qualities representing substantive character. And this form of personal validation is beyond the reach of Herculean efforts to repress women with the intention they have one option to internalize and develop self-perceptions. Possessing nothing but negative experiences that result from the abusive use of power, superiority, and authority renders the Herculean efforts to repress success.

As previously stated, the institution of motherhood provides women with a form of credibility and relevance that is primarily based on *what* they are externally: a mother. However, it is important to realize that acceptance of credibility and relevance on this basis is limited. What are not taken into consideration are qualities that pertain to a woman's personal essence that elevates and distinguishes the difference between being a mother and motherhood. To be a mother principally involves the proficiency to care, nurture, educate, and help develop a child's autonomy and individuality exemplified through inherent qualities that demonstrate their substantive character.

The goal of this system of living is to encourage individuals to be satisfied with achieving credibility and relevance as defined by *what* a person is with respect to external importance and material resources. In this way, it is easier for the elite of any society to dominate the economy, establish cultural standards and practices, as well as devise the political agenda. To bolster the fortitude necessary to triumph over such one-dimensional strategies requires educating a populace to accept a value system that recognizes a person's legitimacy to include the inherent credibility and relevance based on qualities of substantive character.

Jill Mullins, an intersectional feminist, attorney, and activist, gave voice to her opinion in a September 15, 2021, edition of the *Real Change* publication titled: "The Forced-Birth Movement and the Destruction of Our Democracy." She states:

> We have allowed the forced-birth movement to put their feelings over facts. The forced-birth movement uses their belief that an embryo or fetus, a possibility of a life, is as valid as any living, breathing human, to justify the violence they perpetuate in the name of protecting what they believe is "life." Allowing these feelings to justify and normalize violence converted the movement into a terrorist group.
>
> They harass people accessing health care; they assault and even kill providers; they set fire to and even

bomb abortion care facilities. They create crisis pregnancy centers and coerce pregnant people to maintain a pregnancy. The fundamentalist belief of the end justifying the means, including oppressive laws and violence, is one of the reasons our nation is in this perilous moment. The creation of culture wars through abortion has always been a backlash to women of all races and people of color overcoming the original sins of our nation.

Absent from Jill Mullins's editorial is a reminder society cannot legislate morality; however, society can educate to behavior that is moral and ethical. Absent on both sides of the abortion debate is a multidimensional strategy that would benefit society as a whole. Pro-life enthusiasts are invested in a policy that is repressive for the purpose of attaining power, superiority, and authority over what they consider to be a characterless group of women. And the pro-choice enthusiasts are invested in reactionary protesting against their counterparts and rhetoric that "no one shall tell them what to do with their bodies." As mentioned earlier, much needed is a strategy to educate a populace to know and appreciate the essence of human life through the development of substantive character. And without this dedicated social curriculum to train a person to identify, value, and practice qualities of substantive character that establish a moral blueprint, the outcome remains predictable.

Women will remain bitterly divided amongst themselves and, at the same time, hold onto the lie that each is an enemy to another. Historically speaking, the end game is to perpetuate women falling into the trap of being manipulated by power, authority, and dominance to discredit and destroy a woman's autonomy, individuality, and sovereignty. The mishandling of the abortion issue will remain as one of several social ills that impede women—and thus this nation's moral advancement.

We must change the motivation for what fuels self-interest from power, authority, and domination to an opportunity to experience self-interest by dignifying another person's right to execute autonomy and personal authority, which, in turn, honors one's own right to execute autonomy and personal authority. We can experience self-interest by dignifying for every individual the words: "We hold these truths to be self-evident, that all men are created equal, that they are endowed by their Creator with certain unalienable rights, that among these are life, liberty, and the pursuit of happiness."[34]

Jill Filipovic, a Brooklyn-based journalist, lawyer, and author, provides a strong statement that emphasizes the importance of changing the motivation for the perverse usage of self-interest. She states:

> For American women, it throws the future into question: What will it mean to live in a country that has made it clear it doesn't see you as an equal citizen— that doesn't recognize the most basic, intimate right to decide what happens inside your own body? It was never just about abortion. It's about the broader and much more radical cultural shift the reactionary American right wants: a return to traditional gender roles, with men occupying the public, economic, and political spheres, women dependent on men and at home with children.[35]

The lack of appreciation for qualities that represent substantive character has led women, as well as society, to be easily manipulated

---

[34] "The Declaration of Independence," *US National Archives*, https://www.archives.gov/founding-docs/declaration-transcript.

[35] Richard Galant, "Opinion: Supreme Court Mystery Thickens," *CNN.com*, May 8, 2022, https://www.cnn.com/2022/05/08/opinions/supreme-court-roe-v-wade-column-galant/index.html.

by a distorted and perverse masculinity. This distorted and perverted masculinity strictly pursues power, authority, and domination to use against women—and society. The mechanism used to accomplish this goal is evil, which has the intent to discredit and destroy. To trust the confession while enlisting signature attributes such as accountability, forgiveness, compassion, vigilance, and fortitude establishes the seeds of personal empowerment. The time has arrived to stop reacting to the antagonist, be it gender inequality, racism, classism, ageism, and discrimination against sexual orientation.

In order to avoid returning to old traditional gender roles, it will be necessary to trust the confession. This confession is an acknowledgment of a deficiency regarding the education, development, and practice of an individual's most reliable and sustainable value—inherent qualities of representing substantive character. This type of confession is motivated by a buildup of disappointments and emotional pain. The inability to achieve sustainable credibility and relevance within a system of living that encourages individuals of gender, race, class, religion, and family to view one another as bitter rivals generates a great deal of disappointment and emotional pain.

Trust the confession also initiates the process of detaching emotionally, spiritually, and psychologically from a system of living that refuses to acknowledge equal importance to a woman's autonomy, individuality, and credibility as that of her male counterpart. Lastly, this moment of truth creates an opening for a woman to begin the process of self-empowerment through the education, development, and practice of the attributes comprising their inherent value. Men and women unwilling to undergo this transformation from impoverishment to empowerment will continue to attack a woman's autonomy, individuality, and authority based on their internalized self-perception of inferiority. The great English playwright, poet, and actor William Shakespeare set the tone when he stated: "We know what we are but know not what we may be."[36]

---

[36] From William Shakespeare, *Ophelia*. Quoted in *Ophelia Rising*, by Umberto Tosi (Light Fantastic Publishing, 2015).

Chapter 5

GENUINE INTIMACY WILL FACILITATE

Kindness in words creates confidence.
Kindness in thinking creates profoundness.
Kindness in giving creates love.
—Lao Tzu

Talent is cheaper than table salt.
What separates the talented individual
from the successful one
is a lot of hard work.
—Stephen King

When history is banned, stage-managed, forbidden to discuss, or converted to mythologize the past, subsequent environments will have difficulty with the experience of intimacy amongst one another. The inability to prosper from learning of the ill effects that result from intellectual, emotional, and spiritual impoverishment is greatly hampered. It goes without saying a strategy that educates a populace to value and practice traits that represent principles to preserve human life through the development of substantive character is an enormous enterprise. Even though this enterprise is immense, the outcome upon social ills immorally impacting a society will diminish. A reduction in the need for discrimination, injustice, intolerance, and cruelty will allow an opportunity for the populace to be more influenced by a resolute moral foundation.

For example, the education to substantive character allows for the four levels of intimacy to be enacted, which will have a positive influence on the contentious abortion issue. Sharing the same physical space with encouraging results that are supportive for both individuals is the objective of level one. A productive and stimulating exchange of ideas, concepts, and beliefs that can reveal dissimilar intellectual paradigms would describe level two. Being heard without judgment and insensitivity with respect to openness and vulnerability is critical for level three when sharing feelings and emotions relative to past, current, and potential future experiences. Based on the information amassed from the previous three levels, level four provides an opportunity to mutually decide which format the relationship will take on, such as a non-committal acquaintance, friendship, romance with or without a sexual component, or marriage.

With a way of life principally established on inherent credibility and *who* an individual is intrinsically, applying the four levels of intimacy allows for an individual to explore the depths of character prior to deciding whether a protracted friendship or romantic involvement that includes sexual participation is germane. The exploration to identify qualities that comprise the depths of character reveals whether the relationship can be structured on the qualities of integrity, equality, autonomy, individuality, compassion, forgiveness, and community. On the contrary, this exploration can also reveal if the relationship will be structured around power, authority, and self-importance. It is not surprising to know there are individuals who will decide to enter into an imbalanced relationship knowing this particular structure. They are motivated by social validation, economic advantage, fear of being alone, or elation with being part of a community of two.

Also, the information gained from applying the four levels is indispensable when determining whether a casual association, friendship, marriage, or no relationship is appropriate to establish. However, for this analysis, the fourth level of intimacy will be discussed when a long-term friendship—or romantic relationship that includes a sexual component—is a probability. It is true: There are times when individuals who agree to enter into long-term relationships turn out to be one another's worst mortal enemy. Oftentimes, this decision to enter a long-term relationship is made hastily due to an internal need to have a friend or friends in one's life. With respect to a romantic relationship or marriage, unwanted and accidental pregnancies do occur. Utilization of the information made available from each level can help individuals avoid committing prematurely to a sexual and romantic relationship, as well as a marriage that is initiated by internal seduction. To feel loved, wanted, desirable, credible, and relevant are one-dimensional reasons to establish a romantic relationship that includes a sexual component, as well as a marriage.

Instead of allowing the means to justify the end, relevant information pertaining to character and personality is left undisclosed because the end justifies the means. Manipulation to justify establishing a relationship in order to satisfy an internal longing to feel loved and desired can have dire consequences. Motivation to experience redemption, credibility, and relevance will eventually produce a clash between individuals fixated on primarily satisfying their own self-importance and self-indulgence. Relationships structured under these conditions are dominated by which individual can attain the most power, superiority, and authority. Usually, gender, financial position, sex, social standing, physical beauty, and children determine which individual is the more dominant.

Implementing the information emerging from the four levels also helps to safeguard against being swayed by a person's presentation—disguised to look like genuine interest—that instead is based on a selfish intent to use the relationship strictly for utilitarian purposes. Examples of being used for a utilitarian agenda would include interest only in companionship, economic gain, sexual involvement, attraction to physical beauty, a pretense of love, marriage, and raising children for purposes of satisfying a family tradition. There is no genuine interest regarding the other person in the relationship except as a prop to gain credibility and relevance.

Integrity arising from the four levels can protect a person against experiencing, at a future date, the unfavorable consequences of deciding to enter into a relationship primarily based on external and material factors. The prerequisite for any successful relationship—be it causal, friendship, romantic, or marriage—is the application of integrity, especially at the beginning of the relationship. Even though differences will take place more often than not, accountability, kindness, mutual consideration, and personal responsibility ensure a favorable journey for any relationship. It is a wise decision to follow the four levels of intimacy when contemplating whether to pursue a relationship or not.

The first level of intimacy is distinguished by its exploratory effort to determine whether the same physical space can be shared with a person of interest. Attention to equality, autonomy, and individuality—absent an inclination to acquiesce or bloviate—can be explored. The relationship can start out as two individuals coming in contact with one another on an unimaginative basis, such as work, neighborhood store, school, church, or social gathering. In the beginning, conversations can be short, polite, and pedestrian. However, as the occasion of crossing one another's path becomes a recognizable pattern, conversations lengthen, along with a curiosity as to the composition of the individual.

If there are instances when self-importance or boastfulness dominates conversations, uniqueness, autonomy, and equality will not be clearly defined. When this type of interaction becomes a pattern, the relationship is limited when sharing the same physical space. It is important the information revealed not be ignored in order that imbalance does not dictate conditions of the relationship. Furthermore, this information cannot be overlooked for the purpose of defining the relationship parameters, especially when crossing one another's paths on a spontaneous basis. On the other hand, as time continues to reveal a relationship of equality, individuality, and autonomy, and the rise in personal interest continues, a decision becomes imminent. Individually and collectively, the choice to move to level two can be made with mutual consent.

The second level of intimacy is distinguished by the potential to share respective viewpoints and perspectives about life, work, politics, religion, and general beliefs. The exchange provides an expanded window to fathom each individual's personal composition. This is made possible because, up to this point, the relationship has exhibited a capacity for both individuals, independently and collectively, to experience equality, uniqueness, and autonomy. This level of exchange will reveal for the first time disagreements regarding different viewpoints and perspectives, as well as an aptitude to agree to disagree.

The openness to discuss and learn from each other's different viewpoints and attitudes provides an opportunity to develop a more complete portfolio regarding credibility and relevance for each other.

In addition, mutual interest for the other is heightened with autonomy and equality well defined. The absence of an inclination to defer importance to the other or inflate importance to impress the other also becomes defined. With this degree of success and a lack of restrictions, the relationship can be characterized as one of generosity, kindness, admiration, and compassion. Both individuals have a basic feeling of good about the other and self, and both feel good about the overall relationship experience. However, if there is the presence of an inability to experience an openness to discuss and learn from each other's different viewpoints and attitudes, as well as an inability to agree to disagree, the option of going back to level one is always available.

A casual and courteous association can always benefit both individuals. It is imperative to understand that even though individuals involved in this relationship have mutually agreed to move to level two, not everyone is open to sharing respective points of view and attitudes that could be open to discussion. For many individuals, there are long-held generational family viewpoints pertaining to politics, education, religion, abortion, race, and ethnicity that are considered too sacred to have been scrutinized. The aptitude to agree to disagree just isn't there because the will to be right is greater than the will to discuss, learn, and expand one's perceptions. With this information, the relationship can reach its peak at enjoying each other's company but keeping topics of conversation at a non-threatening threshold.

On the other hand, the overall positive experience of level one, along with the personal comfort with different viewpoints and attitudes shared on level two, creates an opportunity for the relationship to advance. A sound decision can be made as to whether level three is a desirable choice. If level three is mutually agreed upon to help develop and strengthen the relationship, both individuals enter a phase when a reciprocal vulnerability is valued and expected. With authenticity and originality already having been demonstrated as principal attributes that establish trust, autonomy, and equality, a defining moment awaits the relationship. This defining moment has a great deal to do with ascertaining whether the relationship can advance to the height of friendship or not. Level three can potentially reveal mutual esteem and affection between two individuals that is more compelling than an interpersonal association.

This level of intimacy is when individuals learn more about the other's character and emotional makeup. The sharing of feelings and emotions pertaining to past and current experiences, both good and otherwise, reveals a depth of character and psychological maturity— or its lack. The difference between the two is that feelings occur in the moment, and emotions represent either mended feelings occurring from learning experiences or feelings that are still active due to experiences remaining internally unresolved. For example, hurt due to rejection can morph into anger if a contributory experience has not been emotionally reconciled. The feeling of elation due to recognition of personal achievement can morph into self-indulgence due to immaturity or be a stage of advancement toward empowerment due to a level of maturity. The sharing of feelings and emotions pertaining to past and current experiences helps to determine how an individual manages and has managed experiences related to personal conflict and success.

This is when each individual will learn about bias, prejudices, what personal conflicts are still alive or have been resolved, and a cultivated victim mentality, if any. Without question, level three will reveal whether the emotional and spiritual aptitude of each person is wrapped too tightly or not around either or both experiences of distress and success. If wrapped too tightly, then there is an indication of an inability to define self-perception separate from experiences culminating in distress or success. An inability to separate oneself emotionally and spiritually from experiences resulting in sorrow or elation creates a condition that will consistently emerge in the future of the relationship—one where the other will be held responsible for either avoiding the recreation of pain or validating the elation. At this point, friendship is difficult to establish. However, still available is the prospect of creating an interpersonal association based on the information revealed in levels one and two.

In contrast, when the third level of intimacy is successful, admiration, affection, gratitude, and a coalition of equals are a fraction of the substantive qualities that emerge in the relationship to bind two individuals. This outcome is not reached in an accelerated fashion because it takes an extended period of time to complete levels one through three. Developing trust takes time to determine whether the compliments, caring, and interest are genuine and based on *who* an individual is intrinsically and not *what* an individual is in terms of external and material factors. To maintain this practice of pursuing authenticity, rather than being lured to a person based on external and material factors, takes courage, stamina, strength, and patience. To allow the initial appeal toward a person to be expanded by an exploration to learn about internal compositions takes staying power to stave off immediate gratification, which can be initially influenced by physical appeal. When relationships are of concern, at times, it will take the full measure of a person to invest in genuineness when living within a system that primarily recognizes external value to be greater than intrinsic value.

With that said, for relationships that are not of a romantic nature, the fourth level of intimacy represents a stage where two individuals are faced with deciding whether or not to move forward with developing an ongoing friendship. Career opportunities, marriage and family responsibilities, or moving to different parts of the globe can impede the emergence of a newly formed meaningful relationship. However, level four represents a stage when another important decision enters the landscape for a potential romantic relationship. For two individuals who have exhibited a commitment to devote time and effort to develop an in-depth portrait of one another, initiating an obligation to protect the relationship requires serious forethought. Having followed levels one through three, both individuals have accumulated significant information regarding themselves and the other. At this point of feeling successful with the discovery, a mutual agreement is reached as to whether sexual involvement is an appropriate component to introduce into the relationship or not.

A truism that has proven itself throughout the generations needs no introduction. When a person is educated to value and practice the qualities that represent their inherent credibility, this same individual embraces the value of human life other than their own. Characteristics such as thoughtfulness, kindness, responsibility, and reliability are essential traits to demonstrate when evaluating one's own commitment to the valued life of another. In other words, for a long-term friendship, a romantic relationship, and marriage to be successful, the qualities that support the credibility and relevance of all individuals involved have to be a priority. The successful achievement of levels one through four verifies the progression that a long-term friendship is possible in spite of differences, a marriage can achieve longevity full of genuine love, and a romantic relationship is possible minus the sexual entanglements. As Helen Keller, the American author, disability rights advocate, political activist, and lecturer, appropriately states: "I would rather walk with a friend in the dark than walk alone in the light."[37]

---

[37] Joseph P. Lash, *Helen and Teacher: The Story of Helen Keller and Anne Sullivan Macey* (United States: Delta/ Seymour Lawrence, 1981), 525.

Ideally, marriage represents the end of a principally established romantic relationship and the commencement of a collaborative effort "till death do you part." Romance, with its allure, passion, and adventure, can certainly be a contributing factor that helps bind the marriage. The information made available through the four levels of intimacy can deepen the appreciation of each other, which includes developing the integral component of love. The four levels of intimacy assist with helping an individual to avoid falling in love, which is a person's internal projection onto the other their perception of being loved. Also occurring within a marriage is the sexual component that consummates an intellectual, emotional, spiritual, and physical union between two individuals.

It is important to remember that a marriage established on the foundation of *who* an individual is intrinsically is more likely to increase its chances for the sexual component to confirm this union rather than being a reward for appeasement. On the other hand, the premature introduction of sex into a relationship can undermine the effort to establish autonomy and equality. It is not uncommon for sex to be used as a weapon by one or both partners to achieve power and domination, which undermines autonomy and equality. Establishing first a friendship, rather than a hastily materialized marriage without the sexual content, can simply be all that the relationship can frame for itself. Just prior to level four, the three preceding levels of intimacy will reveal information that is supportive for both individuals in a meaningful and successful manner.

It is fairly obvious the less a person understands, appreciates, and accepts his or her intrinsic value, the more driven that individual will be to seek worthiness from any external and material means available. It is not uncommon for an individual to be content to wait indefinitely, which the Irish novelist, playwright, and poet Samuel Beckett depicts in *Waiting for Godot*. Originally composed between October 9, 1948, and

January 29, 1949.[38] The two main characters, Vladimir and Estragon, engage each other in numerous conversations centered around the state of affairs pertaining to their respective lives.

Both characters are content to sit and do nothing to personally eliminate the boredom and lack of inspiration that consumes their lives. Both are also waiting for an external and influential source to arrive—that will provide meaning, purpose, salvation, stimulation, and redemption to their lives—who ultimately never arrives. It is important to go slightly beyond Beckett's conclusion. If and when an external and influential source does appear in an individual's life, there is a costly price to pay for the accommodation. The price for providing meaning, purpose, salvation, stimulation, and redemption is the loss of individuality, autonomy, and equality.

A way of life that primarily attaches credibility and relevance based on *what* an individual is in terms of external status and material resources mistakes three peripheral values as invaluable. Sex is equated with love, career and money are equated with security and worth, and beauty with prominence. When personally committed to this way of life, level four of intimacy is commonly reversed to become level one. Decisions involving sex, marriage, and having children are often made, having been influenced by reversing the beneficial order of the four levels of intimacy. The outcome of this type of decision-making process is to establish a way of life based on power, authority, and prominence.

Another glaring issue that arises when predominantly relying on external and material factors to attain credibility and relevance is dependency. This particular way of life creates a personal need to have an outside source be responsible for one's own well-being, as portrayed in *Waiting for Godot*. A common approach adopted toward living one's life is to pursue sex and other external means to satisfy what is a fundamental internal state of emotional and spiritual impoverishment.

---

[38] Samuel Beckett, *Waiting for Godot* (New York: Grove Press, 1954).

The need to satisfy a ravenous appetite to be valued, seen, and heard becomes a consistent denominator with a way of life principally based on attaining external status and material worth. Under these circumstances, associations, relationships and especially marriage have a difficult time being successful when power, authority, and domination are the end goals. Conversely, with a way of life based on *who* an individual is innately, associations, relationships, and especially marriage experience a high degree of success. Why? Because the personal sense of completeness and value originates from within the individual. Developing associations, relationships, and marriage that honor autonomy, individuality, and equality are an end goal, and the four levels of intimacy help to accentuate this reality.

Placing an early emphasis on learning as much as possible with respect to the internal content of a potential partner can eliminate periods of discomfort later in a relationship. When the reason for forming a relationship is primarily based on external status and material resources, surprises that can be disruptive to the bond await the unsuspected. Minimizing effort and time to develop an emotional, intellectual, and spiritual portrait of a potential partner can lead to unreconciled experiences inadvertently emerging that cause one or the other to be subjected to unsettled pain. Past experiences culminating in neglect, abuse, rejection, overindulgence, and entitlement that remain emotionally unresolved are often projected onto the partner by means of anger, rage, or a lack of civility.

Because the effort and time to develop an in-depth portrait of a prospective partner have been minimized, levels two and three cannot be successfully satisfied. Due to a deficiency pertaining to inherent credibility and related qualities, negative experiences that have remained unresolved leave an individual with one option to define oneself. That one option to develop self-perception is through good, bad, or indifferent experiences. Surprises await the unsuspected when one or more experiences suddenly take center stage in the relationship when unsettled internal content has been consciously awakened.

As earlier stated, unresolved experiences such as neglect, abuse, rejection, and overindulgence can revisit a partner during an unsuspecting and innocent event. Serious setbacks for a relationship or marriage occur when an in-depth portrait of a prospective partner is minimized. This type of episode generally takes place when a relationship or marriage is forced because the initial attraction is based on external and material factors. The end justifies the means, which oftentimes occurs when sexual involvement replaces exploring levels one through three on a more comprehensive basis.

Investing in *what* an individual is strictly defined by external and material benchmarks without investing in knowing *who* that person is as distinguished by the attributes comprising inherent credibility provides a valid reason why practices of discrimination, injustice, intolerance, and cruelty have continuously represented a symptomatic social ill. There is a lack of accountability from the populace regarding the adverse influence of self-importance and self-indulgence when making determinations that devalue human life. When a person is exposed to substantive character development, that individual is also exposed to moral and ethical standards. Teach a person to appreciate and value the best attributes they bring into this world and that appreciation and value is reflected pertaining to decisions that impact the social community as a whole.

As a people, we are encouraged to trust one another with our aspirations, frailties, loyalty, triumphs, affection, and support. The dilemma that arises alongside this encouragement to be vulnerable is that, as a people, we reside within a system of living devoid of the incentive to personally recognize, value, and practice the qualities that represent substantive character.

Under these circumstances that instead foster developing an awareness and pursuit of personal recognition based on power, authority, and prominence, it is more prudent to trust the act of good rather than the person. Credibility, relevance, and value experienced on both sides of the relationship will be an act of good to trust. It takes a lifetime of making mistakes with respect to whom to trust and learning from those mistakes to grasp the difference between entrusting power, authority, and prominence and the act of good when the issue of trust is involved.

—Lorenzo D. Leonard

Chapter 6

HISTORY THAT IS WRITTEN

Considerable interest is created when listening to the loud and alarming exclamations from the media, Democratic politicians, and portions of this nation's populace the US democracy is under attack. The cries proclaim, "Our democracy is in peril." Its existence is in danger of collapsing if nothing is done to protect the four indispensable elements of democracy. Larry Diamond, a political sociologist and leading contemporary scholar in the field of democratic studies, applicably details its four indispensable elements.

Diamond describes democracy as a system of government with four key elements:

1. A system for choosing and replacing the government through free and fair elections.
2. Active participation of the people, as citizens, in politics and civic life.
3. Protection of the human rights of all citizens.
4. A rule of law in which the laws and procedures apply equally to all citizens.

The interest expressed in the opening paragraph has to do with an overlooked precedent created when our forefathers implemented the US democracy. The need to discuss this precedent is to reveal when our democracy came under attack and in peril. To intentionally exclude millions of individuals living in America from experiencing the four elements indispensable for the longevity and success of democracy exposed an unprincipled republic. America's founding documents lacked a moral blueprint and epitomized nothing more than a Sunday morning church sermon. The occasion for the documents to exemplify a moral blueprint was lost when the Founding Fathers decided the rights of minorities should not equal the rights of the wealthy and property owners.

James Madison, in his August 7, 1787, publicized speech at the Federal Convention titled "The Right of Suffrage," clearly expresses this position. Madison stated:

> The right of suffrage is a fundamental Article in Republican constitutions. The regulation of it is, at the same time, a task of peculiar delicacy. Allow the right exclusively to property, and the rights of persons may be oppressed. The feudal polity alone sufficiently proves it. Extend it equally to all, and the rights of property or the claims of justice may be overruled by a majority without property or interested in measures of injustice. Of this abundant proof is afforded by other popular governments and is not without examples in our own, particularly in the laws impairing the obligation of contracts.[39]

---

[39] "The Founders' Constitution," Volume 1, Chapter 16, Document 26, *Documentary History of the Constitution of the United States of America, 1786–1870*, 5 vols (Washington, D.C.: Department of State, 1901).

Rather than take responsibility as governmental leaders of a new republic and extend an equal right of suffrage and citizenship to all inhabitants of America, the Founding Fathers passed their authority on to a third party. The Founding Fathers were distinctly reluctant to needlessly place their wealth and power in jeopardy by passing equal rights legislation for voting and citizenship. The two responsibilities were passed on to the states to determine through what turned out to be oppressive constitutions and laws. The age-old idiom that captures the Founding Fathers' political maneuver is commonly referred to as "kicking the can down the road for someone else to figure out a solution." Initially excluded from experiencing the indispensable elements of a US democracy were women, Native Americans, Blacks, and other minority groups.

Nell Irvin Painter, a leading historian of the United States and a retiree from Princeton University as the Edwards Professor of American History Emerita, states in her book, *The History of White People*:

> The (United States) government of this new republic went about its own mundane business, answering its own questions by counting its people according to its own devices. In article 1, sections 2 and 9 of the Constitution, the United States created a novel way of apportioning representation and direct taxation: a national census every ten years. The first US census, taken in 1790, recognized six categories within the population: (1) the head of each household, (2) free white males over sixteen, (3) free white males under sixteen, (4) free white females, (5) all other free persons by sex and color, and (6) slaves.[40]

---

[40] Nell Irvin Painter, *The History of White People* (New York: W.W. Norton & Company, 2010), 180.

Another Founding Father, George Washington, was displeased with the eighteen-month effort to accurately count the inhabitants of America, which in numerous political camps throughout the globe viewed Americans as white. The census counted 3.9 million people, which George Washington exclaimed was "too low." Painter goes on to state:

> Three terms parsed the only race—white—and two categories demarcated slave and free legal statuses. Unfree white persons, of whom there were many in the new union, seem to have fallen through the cracks in 1790, though the fourfold mention of the qualifier "free" by inference recognizes the non-free white status of those in servitude. Had all whites been free and whiteness meant freedom, as is often assumed today, no need would have existed to add "free" to "white."[41]

For the Founding Fathers, there existed less of a threat from "free" Americans regarding a revolt against their wealth and property. "Free" Americans would be too focused on exercising their superiority and privilege, as well as acquiring their own wealth and property. Rather than being overly concerned with the Founding Fathers' wealth and property, attention to fulfilling their own self-interest became a priority. Voting rights, citizenship, and superiority would embolden the preeminence of being considered "true Americans." Painter continues:

> Census categories kept changing every ten years, as governmental needs changed and taxonomical categories shifted, including taxonomies of race. [Taxonomy is the science of naming, describing, and classifying

---

[41] Painter, *The History*, 105.

organisms.] Congress counted all the free persons (women, too, although they did not have the right to vote) and three-fifths of 'others,' that is, indentured laborers and slaves. As politics freed all white people and ideology whitened the face of freedom, 'free white males' seemed a useless redundancy. The abolition of economic barriers to voting by white men made the United States, in the then common parlance, 'a white man's country,' a polity defined by race and limited to white men. Once prerequisites for active citizenship came down to maleness and whiteness, poor men could be welcomed into the definition of American, if they could be defined as white—the first enlargement of American whiteness.[42]

The Founding Fathers—who represented political, legislative, and economic authority to avoid declaring the right of suffrage to all inhabitants of America in order to protect their wealth and power—put the US democracy in a state of mere theory at the start of its existence. The fear that fellow Americans in subordinate economic and social positions could revolt and strip away their wealth and property was just too much for the Founding Fathers to place in jeopardy. Established at the beginning of this republic was an example of when personal interest took precedence over the moral authority and credibility of the nation.

This choice shattered the hope of beginning this republic on principles representative of a moral blueprint. Self-interest got in the way of a highly intelligent group of men understanding "the smallest deed is better than the grandest intention." Once more, there is the reminder that wealth, power, and elitism will never expunge emotional, spiritual, and psychological impoverishment. And as with

---

[42] Painter, *The History*, 106.

most endeavors at its beginning, failure to formulate and commit to establishing a foundation built on a moral blueprint swiftly creates the basis for an eventual collapse.

This example, advanced by the Founding Fathers, became a template for others to follow as the republic opened its doors of inclusion to include more "males" who were "white." The US democracy was created in the beginning and afterward to primarily serve only the "white male," for some "white males" to this very day consider themselves "true Americans." As this framework developed, so did the need to develop the lethal practice of economic, social, educational, housing, employment, and religious discrimination. From the beginning of the US democracy, the need to protect against any group or individual attempting to usurp the wealth, power, and dominance of the "white male" has been considered a life and death issue. Privilege, entitlement, wealth, and property are not to be shared on an equal and equivalent basis with any group or individual.

The archives of this nation's history have revealed the US democracy's lack of integrity and state of impoverishment. It would not be until August 18, 1920, when Congress ratified the Nineteenth Amendment to the US Constitution, that all women were guaranteed the right to vote. On June 2, 1924, Congress passed the Indian Citizenship Act for all Native Americans born in the United States; however, it would not be until the early sixties when Native Americans were granted the right to vote. The Fourteenth Amendment was ratified by Congress on July 9, 1868, which granted citizenship to all persons "born or naturalized in the United States," including formerly enslaved people. In addition, this amendment provided all citizens with "equal protection under the laws." The Fifteenth Amendment further states, "The right of citizens of the United States to vote shall not be denied or abridged by the United States or by any state on account of race, color, or previous condition of servitude."

The Fifteenth Amendment guaranteed Black American men the right to vote. However, the Fifteenth Amendment had a clever escape clause to protect the rich, prominent, and powerful. Cunningly, the amendment did not grant suffrage to all men but only prohibited discrimination based on race and former slave status. States could require voters to pass literacy tests, pay poll taxes, be subjected to the grandfather clause, or outright intimidation. Such burdens and the corresponding experiences were extremely difficult for the formerly enslaved to overcome with limited income, education, and advocacy.

To put an end to the legal obstacles at the state and local levels that prevented African Americans from exercising their right to vote as guaranteed under the Fifteenth Amendment, President Lyndon B. Johnson signed into law the 1965 Voting Rights Act. This amendment outlawed the discriminatory voting practices adopted in many Southern states after the Civil War. In actuality, the Voting Rights Act of 1965 was a political maneuver to enforce the Fifteenth Amendment to the Constitution ninety-five years after being ratified and signed into law. To his very day, this act remains the most sweeping and comprehensive civil rights legislation in the history of the United States.

The early history of America reveals two important events that helped to distinctly shape self-perceptions of privilege and entitlement. It is well known the wealthy and powerful Founding Fathers of America reviled the tyrannical rule of the British government. However, when establishing the American government, these elite men would commit a serious error of judgment or "cardinal sin" that would initiate for the American populace a path of damnation. This path would come to be the beginning when Americans would fight with one another for power, authority, and prominence over one another. Income, gender, race, ethnic, educational, religious, age, and reproductive decision inequalities would become issues of contention.

The Founding Fathers failed to establish a system of living in America based on the principles of moral authority, integrity, and a coalition of equals. Because of this failure, these men were left with no other option than to become examples for other Americans to follow. The Founding Fathers would illustrate for Americans the abuse of power, authority, and prominence just as their English oppressive predecessors had exemplified. This was the first event in American history that distinctly shaped self-perceptions of privilege and entitlement.

The second important event that helped to distinctly shape self-perceptions of privilege and entitlement by the Founding Fathers was to duplicate disingenuous behavior, again just as their English oppressive predecessors did when establishing American colonies. The practices of discrimination and injustice that were committed against women, the BIPOC communities, the poor, and cultures not fluent speaking English prevented these groups of Americans from experiencing the right to life, liberty, and the pursuit of happiness. This failure by the Founding Fathers to establish a moral blueprint for America to begin its existence and for all Americans to replicate spoke volumes regarding the self-indulgence of the elite that generated self-perceptions of privilege and entitlement.

These two events were held by former President Donald Trump, numerous Trump supporters, the Capitol rioters, and their predecessors as reasonable justifications for the assault upon the United States Capitol in Washington, DC, on January 6, 2021. There is an explicit connection between former President Donald Trump and a vast number of people who cast their votes for him to be president. The attack on the Capitol was conducted by individuals familiar with America's opening history. Outside of the rioters, it is logical to assume that many Trump voters were familiar with this history as well. And it is also rational to assume that many of these same voters and participants in the Capitol assault were aware the US democracy is nothing more than a "paper tiger." It is no secret to this group—comprised of discontent descendants who, along with their predecessors, had enjoyed an economic and social benefit from a democracy—that the United States, from its beginning, had been slanted to serve their faction of the American population.

The attack on the United States Capitol was an expression of their extreme discontent and dislike with losing their unparalleled privilege and entitlement to factions of the populace originally denied the right to vote and own property. When the Founding Fathers chose, for all to see, personal interest taking precedence over the moral authority expressed in the Declaration of Independence, the US democracy was reduced to a mere abstract theory. This perception of superiority was made blatantly clear with the March 6, 1857, United States Supreme Court Dred Scott decision. The court ruled that the Declaration of Independence and the rights guaranteed by the Constitution did not apply to Negroes and never had.[43] Even though Scott had fled a slave state to live in a free state and territory, as an enslaved individual, he was still the property of his enslaver. Therefore, because Scott was not a free man, he was not a citizen of America, and nor could he sue in Federal Court.[44]

Though these events have been briefly discussed, the subject deserves further elaboration to disclose a significant contradiction the English immigrants failed to correct. History has revealed England wanted to start an American colony to increase its wealth and power. This additional wealth was thought to be necessary to compete with other European countries, namely Spain and France, for resources

---

[43] "Dred Scott vs. Stanford, 60 US 393 (1856)," *Justia US Supreme Court*, accessed May 10, 2022, https://supreme.justia.com/cases/federal/us/60/393/.

[44] Melvin I. Urofsky, "Dred Scott Decision," *Britannica*, accessed May 10, 2022, https://www.britannica.com/event/Dred-Scott-decision.

such as gold, silver, and furs. The term "colony" was ascribed to the expedition because the British immigrants who came to America were under the total authority of England.

The primary reason why English immigrants welcomed the journey to America was to escape the harsh economic, political, and religious conditions in Britain. The colonial population in America grew from about 2,000 to 2.4 million between 1625 and 1775, when multiple colonies were established. Thirteen British colonies were established during the seventeenth and early eighteenth centuries in the eastern United States. The upper colonies were New Hampshire, Massachusetts (Maine was part of the colony), Rhode Island, and Connecticut. The middle colonies were New Jersey, New York, Delaware, and Pennsylvania. The Southern colonies were Maryland, Virginia, Carolina (In 1729 split into North and South), and Georgia.

It is true that many English immigrants came to America seeking religious freedom, but there were many who were seeking their personal fortune, individual recognition, and singular glory. At the start of colony life, the colonists governed themselves following the laws as dictated by the English Parliament and maintained their loyalty to King George III. In general, the colonists enjoyed a great deal of religious, financial, political, and personal freedom; however, over a period, the expected strict obedience by colonists to parliamentary authority began to deteriorate. Unreasonable expectations, demands, and outrageous legislation in the form of taxes eventually became viable reasons for the colonists to end British control over them and start a way of life based strictly on their distinct sovereignty.

A point had been reached when it was no longer acceptable for colonists to embrace legislation authorized by King George III and the British Parliament. For example, colonies were forced to primarily rely on Britain for imported goods and supplies due to a trade restriction. To make economic conditions worse, there were no banks and very little money, so colonists used barter and credit to purchase goods and services. Legislation established in Britain made colonists responsible for finding or paying for the lodging expenses of British soldiers. This became completely intolerable upon the realization the British military held the power to give orders, make decisions, and enforce obedience involving the colonists as authorized by a distant authority. The thinking amongst the colonies was quite clear; any military force not authorized by the colonial government had no jurisdiction over the colonists.

The English Parliament decided to implement different tax amendments to help pay off war debts that occurred while fighting the French and Native Americans. One tax imposed upon the colonists was the Stamp Act, passed in 1765, which required the use of special paper bearing an embossed tax stamp for all legal documents. Another tax was the Townshend Acts, passed in 1767, which required the colonists to pay taxes on imported goods, such as tea from China. The immediate reaction of the colonists was negative in tone and behavior. The idea and implementation of the new taxes that originated with the British Parliament and not from the colonial governments ignited much debate across the colonies.

The thought of being required to pay taxes to a distant British government while experiencing no representation was simply "a bridge too far" for the colonists. As for Englishmen, this was a clear violation of their basic rights. Protests quickly developed in the form of boycotting—or not buying British goods. To further demonstrate their displeasure with mounting taxes, the Sons of Liberty in Boston, Massachusetts, boarded ships on December 16, 1773, dressed as Native Americans and hurled imported tea into the water. Protesters had successfully prevented the unloading of tea in three other colonies. This historical event is referred to as the Boston Tea Party, which was a political and trade protest against King George III and the British Parliament.

In retaliation, the king and parliament ordered the British navy to put in place a blockade of the Boston Harbor. In addition, parliament passed retaliatory legislation known as the *Intolerable Acts*. The motivation for the English monarchy and government to create the laws was to punish the Massachusetts colonists for their hostile and belligerent behavior pertaining to the Tea Party revolt. The British government understood quite well the primary reason for the protest was the implementation of tougher legislation. The punishment was extended to include the suppression of the Massachusetts colonists' and other colonies' right to self-governance enjoyed from the beginning of colonial life.

Resistance to parliamentary authority by the colonies had begun to increase since the enactment of the American Revenue (Sugar) Tax of April 5, 1764. This tax was British Parliament's attempt to increase revenue by imposing taxes and regulations on goods imported into the colonies, such as molasses and sugar. By singling out the Massachusetts colonists with punitive measures for the Boston revolt, the British Parliament had hoped the colonial resistance would simply go away. Instead, tensions escalated between the opposing parties, which necessitated the colonists to gather as one organized group. The First Continental Congress was assembled to assure their efforts to address grievances against the British would not be excessive or forcibly stated.

There were colonists who wanted to remain loyal to the king and British Parliament. At this time in world history, Britain was the most powerful empire in the global community. Not everyone throughout the colony community was enthusiastic about taking on what appeared to be overwhelming odds against securing their independence from a massive opponent. In spite of this passiveness, this cautious approach would not be an adequate maneuver to satisfy one individual in particular. Thomas Jefferson would unpredictably distinguish himself as a clever and competent political writer by his colleagues with his response to King George III and the British Parliament.

In 1774, Jefferson completed writing his blistering rebuttal to King George III and parliament's punitive reactions to the colonists—especially participants of the Boston Tea Party. The title of his rebuff was "A Summary View of the Rights of British America." According to Rodger D. Parker, author of Wellsprings of a Nation: America before 1801, aside from the declaration, this treatise was "the greatest literary contribution to the American Revolution."[45] Written several months prior, the summary was the forerunner to Thomas Jefferson's first draft of the US Declaration of Independence.

The highly charged summary consisted of grievances and objections against the five legislative acts that were to be followed by the colonists. Jefferson responded to the entire package of legislation, referred to as the "Intolerable Acts." The legislation included the Boston Port Act, the Massachusetts Government Act, the Administration of Justice Act, the Quartering Act, and expanding the borders of the Quebec Act into America. Without question, the regulations placed harsher restrictions on the colonies. For example, the justice system developed within the colonies was forced to capitulate its authority and submit to the absolute rule of British authority.

---

[45] Roger D. Parker, *Wellsprings of a Nation: America Before 1801: A Bicentennial Exhibition from the Collections of the America Antiquarian Society at the Worcester Art Museum* (Worcester, MA: American Antiquarian Society, 1977).

Jefferson's argument for colonial independence was designed to emphasize the fundamentals of "natural law." Each colony was individually established; the colonists owned the land, which included constructed buildings and add-on fixtures. Under such conditions, the "natural law" of independence becomes self-evident. Due to this inherent state of independence, Jefferson concluded the British Parliament had no authority to tax, establish a military presence, or govern the colonies. He states in his summary:

> America was conquered, and her settlements made, and firmly established, at the expense of individuals, and not of the British public. Their own blood was spilt in acquiring lands for their settlements, their own fortunes expended in making that settlement effectual; for themselves they fought, for themselves they conquered, and for themselves alone they have right to hold. No shilling was ever issued from the public treasures of His Majesty, or his ancestors, for their assistance.[46]

Jefferson provided a detailed analysis and ultimate rejection of each punitive legislative act that would prove British strategies were devious and unethical. As stated earlier, his masterstroke statement, "The British Parliament has no right to exercise authority over us," would be repeated after addressing each act. Because the American colonies were independently established, no feudal system existed. Neither King George III nor the British Parliament served as landlords providing land to Americans in exchange for their loyalty and service. It is true that British rule was pervasive throughout the

---

[46] Scott J. Hammond, Kevin R. Hardwick, Howard L. Lubert, *Classics of American Political and Constitutional Thought, Volume 1* (Indianapolis: Hackett Publishing, 2007), 250.

colonies in the beginning but in a limited format. But as "natural law" came to exist due to the colonies developing more and more autonomy in terms of government, politics, economics, social, and religious perspectives, British rule was viewed as less and less relevant.

It is of interest to note that Thomas Jefferson also devoted a segment of his summary to expressing his condemnation of slavery to King George III. At the young age of thirty-three years old and several weeks later, Jefferson would express the same sentiment in a 168-word passage he initially included in his first draft of the Declaration of Independence. Jefferson's intent in each document was to blame King George III for Britain's support and continuance of slavery as one of the many grievances the colonies had against them. He states in the Summary View of the Rights of British America:

> The Middle Passage—the transporting of slaves from West Africa to British colonies in the Caribbean, South America, Central America, and the thirteen American colonies violates the most sacred right of life and liberty in the persons of a distant people who never offended him (King George III), captivating and carrying them into slavery. The king has waged cruel war against human nature itself, violating the most sacred right of life and liberty in the persons of a distant people.[47]

Thomas Jefferson was en route to the Virginia Convention of 1774 to present his Summary View of the Rights of British America. However, while traveling, Jefferson became ill and was unable to attend the Virginia Convention to present the treatise to his fellow

---

[47] Ed. Julian P. Boyd, *The Papers of Thomas Jefferson Vol. 1, 1760–1776* (Princeton: Princeton University Press, 1950), 243–247.

delegates for their approval. Committed to not miss this opportunity, he was able to send a written statement in support of his summary. After a prolonged discussion among the Virginia representatives, the treatise was thought to be highly provocative by a majority attending the convention.

Clementina Rind, a woman from Williamsburg, Virginia, and a supporter of Jefferson, was not to be deterred. She made a print of the summary and provided Patrick Henry with one copy to take to the Continental Congress, which met in Philadelphia, Pennsylvania, from September 5 to October 26, 1774. The treatise was read and debated among the fifty-six delegates, twelve of the thirteen British colonies (the state of Georgia did not attend). At the conclusion of the debate, congressional delegates decided to soften their response to King George III and parliament.

The overall reaction to Jefferson's summary was that he was far too radical, and a moderate approach would be more appropriate. As previously stated, loyalty to the king and British Parliament remained an important issue for many colonists. In addition, challenging the world's most powerful empire just did not seem like a prudent idea. At this time in world history, Britain was the most powerful empire in the global community. For Jefferson, the realization that his competent writing skills and electrifying rhetoric were not enough for many congressional members to change their decision from a moderate to a radical retort to King George III and parliament was a personal letdown. But, despite this disappointment and defeat, Jefferson was delighted that sympathetic friends printed the treatise and distributed copies throughout Philadelphia, New York, London, and much of what soon would become the United States.

Later in the year, the preselected committee chosen by the Second Continental Congress to edit the first draft of Thomas Jefferson's

Declaration of Independence included John Adams (New England), Benjamin Franklin (Pennsylvania), and Robert Livingston (New York). This committee removed the 168 antislavery word passages from the document's final wording. The delegations of South Carolina and Georgia strongly objected to the passage condemning slavery. There arises the thought of measured aversion that Thomas Jefferson may have used the slavery passages in both documents to divert blame away from colonists who were slave owners.

It was accepted hypocrisy that many of the colonists who sought freedom from British tyranny themselves bought and sold human beings. The interest that is generated by Jefferson's condemnation of slavery arises from the fact that he was a lifelong slave owner. What intensifies the interest is that during Jefferson's lifetime, he owned over 600 enslaved people—more than any United States president. Of US presidents who owned slaves, George Washington was close behind Jefferson. On Thomas Jefferson's deathbed, he ignored the wishes of friends and family to free his slaves. Of the 600 enslaved people he owned, Jefferson freed only ten people during his life, and all ten were members of the same family.[48]

> After Peter Jefferson died in 1757, his estate was divided between his sons Thomas and Randolph. Thomas inherited approximately 5,000 acres (2,000 ha; 7.8 sq. mi.) of land, including Monticello. He assumed full authority over his property at age 21. Jefferson also inherited fifty-two slaves. In 1768, Jefferson began construction of his Monticello plantation. Through his marriage to Martha Wayles in

---

[48] Lina Mann, "The Enslaved Household of President Thomas Jefferson," *The White House Historical Society*, accessed May 10, 2022, https://www.whitehouse-history.org/slavery-in-the-thomas-jefferson-white-house

1772 and inheritance from his father-in-law John Wayles in 1773, Jefferson inherited two plantations and 135 more slaves. By 1776, Jefferson was one of the largest planters in Virginia.

Thomas Jefferson's statement pertaining to slavery in his Summary View of the Rights of British America is as follows:

> The abolition of domestic slavery is the great object of desire in those colonies, where it was unhappily introduced in their infant state. But previous to the enfranchisement of the slaves we have, it is necessary to exclude all further importations from Africa; yet our repeated attempts to affect this by prohibitions, and by imposing duties which might amount to a pro-hibition, have been hitherto defeated by His Majesty's negative:

> Thus, preferring the immediate advantages of a few African corsairs to the lasting interests of the American states, and to the rights of human nature, deeply wounded by this infamous practice. Nay, the single interposition of an interested individual against a law was scarcely ever known to fail of success, though in the opposite scale were placed the interests of a whole country. That this is so shameful an abuse of a power trusted with His Majesty for other pur-poses, as if not reformed, would call for some legal restrictions.[49]

To understand Jefferson's contrasting positions, it is important to examine his background. The economic historians Eric McKitrick

---

[49] Hammond, et al., *Classics*, 254.

and Stanley Elkins state in their book, The Age of Federalism: The Early American Republic, 1788–1800:

> Jefferson's rise (to prominence) was swift and smooth as leaders of the provincial elite quickly recognized his abilities and in effect brought him into the ruling group while still in his mid-twenties. The coercions of this insider-ship were undoubtedly considerable. The system had given him everything he could have asked for: wealth, love and a profitable marriage, social position, the fullest opportunity to engage his talents, and general recognition. He was thus allowed the luxury of determining which of these things he valued the most, and which least, without having to give up any of them. Such being the case, the likelihood of his offering a basic challenge to that system, whatever the defects he might decide needed remedying, was not very great. He might suppose himself viewing it with detachment, but he would never do so from the outside.[50]

The month of April in 1775 was the month American colonies would officially break with British control. On April 14, the newly appointed British governor of Massachusetts, General Gage, was ordered by his superiors to "use any force necessary to apply all British acts and to stop any buildup of a colonial militia."[51] Many historians believe the Battles of Lexington and Concord on April 18 and 19 to

---

[50] Eric McKitrick and Stanley Elkins, *The Age of Federalism: The Early American Republic, 1788–1800* (New York: Oxford University Press, 1993), 204.

[51] Martin Kelly, "Major Events That Led to the American Revolution," *ThoughtCo*, November 4, 2020, https://www.thoughtco.com/timeline-events-leading-to-american-revolution-104296.

be the actual dates the American Revolution began. The colonists turned back the British attempt to destroy its arms depot in Concord, Massachusetts. The American Revolutionary War began in April 1775, and the United States of America declared its independence from British rule in July 1776.

Thomas Jefferson's political stance that the colonists had an inherent right to reject the British government's authority and establish their own government was based on a statement that, at first glance, fashioned the Declaration of Independence as a moral mission statement. The statement, "All men are created equal and have the inalienable rights of life, liberty, and the pursuit of happiness," was in reference to the colony men who were lawyers, political leaders, farmers of tobacco, slave owners, land investors, and entrepreneurs.

Women, the poor and uneducated, Native Americans, and about one-fifth of the population that consisted of Black Americans were all deprived of their own "inalienable" right to liberty. It is quite evident from this untold history regarding the birth of America that the "Founding Fathers were fighting for freedom—just not for everyone."[52] As previously stated, for Black Americans, this perception was made clear with the March 6, 1857, US Supreme Court Dred Scott decision that "the Declaration of Independence and the rights guaranteed by the Constitution did not apply to Negroes and never had."

For the Founding Fathers to remain self-indulgent and silent regarding discrimination committed against women, genocide against Native Americans, slavery of Black people, and inequities exerted against the poor and educated generated centuries of struggle within America over basic human and civil rights. To fight for independence against King George III and the British Parliament while denying a

---

[52] Yohuru Williams, "Why Thomas Jefferson's Anti-slavery Passage Was Removed from the Declaration of Independence, *History.com*, June 29, 2020, https://www.history.com/news/declaration-of-independence-deleted-anti-slavery-clause-jefferson.

vast number of Americans their inalienable right to life, liberty, and the pursuit of happiness and freedom propelled a "US Democracy into peril." All of this early American history demonstrated when self-interest and self-importance were considered more important than demonstrating moral authority. This example was the fodder that initiated the rise of gender, racial, ethnic, economic, social, and educational injustices throughout America based on a perverse sense of privilege and entitlement stimulated by an emotional, intellectual, and spiritual impoverishment.

The impoverishment in question is a lack of understanding and appreciation regarding a person's inherent credibility, relevance, and value that embodies their true worth. Trust the confession that one does not know how to live their personal life based on the qualities that represent a meritorious character. This confession allows an individual to begin the process of detaching emotionally, psychologically, and spiritually from a system of living that ignores the education and development of an individual's innate value. This current system promotes impoverishment because it strictly bases legitimacy on power and authority, attained primarily on external sources and material acquisitions.

The outward manifestations generated from this way of life are to induce the populace to fight and destroy one another for the "breadcrumbs" of impoverishment. The sporadic droppings of small morsels that represent an artificial sense of credibility intensify an internal state of impoverishment. Remember, evil is the outward display of emotional, intellectual, and spiritual impoverishment. Trust the confession to move from fear of vulnerability and its representative to a full embrace. Disavow this ignorance of one's innate credibility and relevance in exchange for personal freedom that is exemplified by substantive character.

The former President Donald Trump, his supporters, the Capitol rioters, a dysfunctional government, a political system that lacks moral leadership, the abortion crisis, and the rise in indiscriminate hatred and violence throughout America are examples of this impoverishment. The American history just revisited is the one most read and learned, absent the two critical events that have kept this democracy representing nothing more than a "paper tiger." The first critical event has just been discussed, while the second event is forthcoming in more detail within the next chapter.

Chapter 7

THE NATION IS HONEST, TRUTHFUL, AND VIRTUOUS

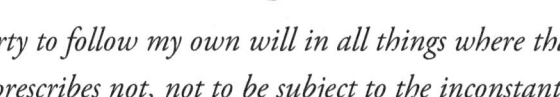

*A liberty to follow my own will in all things where that
rule prescribes not, not to be subject to the inconstant,
uncertain, unknown, arbitrary will of another
man, as freedom of nature is to be under
no other restraint but the law of Nature.*
—John Locke

*I prefer liberty with danger than peace with slavery.
Man is born free, and everywhere he is in chains.
People in their natural state are basically good.
But this natural innocence, however, is
corrupted by the evils of society.*
—Jean-Jacques Rousseau

The following is an expanded version of a statement used in previously authored publications. This expanded version describes the importance of being able to reason backwards to resolve what, on the surface, may appear complicated. Sir Arthur

Conan Doyle was a British writer and physician. Doyle was primarily recognized for creating the popular fictional character Sherlock Holmes, who was an unrivaled detective when solving complicated crimes. His steadfast friend Dr. Watson assisted Holmes on many instances in solving cryptic and complex crimes. On one occasion, Watson found himself on the receiving end of a profound revelation after the detective solved a thorny and mysterious crime. The forthcoming revelation began when Watson stated to his friend, "Holmes, how did you solve this mystery with so many unscripted developments?"

Holmes calmly replied,

> My dear friend Watson, in solving a problem of this sort, the grand thing is to be able to reason backwards. That is a very useful accomplishment, and a very easy one, but people do not practice it much. In the everyday affairs of life, it is more useful to reason forwards, and so the other comes to be neglected. There are fifty who can reason synthetically for one who can reason analytically . . . Let me see if I can make it clearer. Most people, if you describe a train of events to them, will tell you what the result would be. They can put those events together in their minds and argue from them that something will come to pass. There are few people, however, who, if you told them a result, would be able to evolve from their own inner consciousness what the steps were which led up to that result. This power is what I mean when I talk of reasoning backwards, or analytically.[53]

---

[53] Sir Arthur Conan Doyle, *A Study in Scarlet* (UK: Delphi Classics, 2017).

A strategy that educates the American populace to value and preserve human life based on studying and embracing the attributes that represent substantive character is an enormous enterprise to undertake. To replace the current system of living that began with the commencement of humankind and later reinforced with the inception of this nation will not be an accepted strategy. The obstacle preventing this modification from occurring is an entrenched custom that promotes the idea human life has little value and, for that reason, does not qualify to be preserved. The firewall that protects this custom is an ideology that proclaims how the attainment of personal credibility and relevance is achieved by exerting one's self-will over another person or group to attain power, authority, and prominence. Daily, this custom can be attested to throughout societal institutions such as the economy, government, workplace, marriage, family, community, athletics, social media, military, religion, politics, various races, and ethnicities.

For very good reason, during an individual's developmental years, six to nineteen years of age, the education to identify and practice qualities linked to virtuous character is not promoted as a crucial pathway to self-empowerment. The development of personal autonomy, individuality, and innate intelligence are characteristics that safeguard an individual from internalizing the experience of being terrorized by another individual's display of self-will. A system of living that promotes the achievement of personal legitimacy based on exerting self-will over another person or group to attain power, authority, and prominence is not interested in the development of self-empowerment. The term carries with it a compelling undertone that economic, social, and religious imbalances of power and authority could be in jeopardy of losing their stranglehold on immorality. For individuals and groups who have benefited from advances gained by the unethical use of power, authority, and prominence, this is an intolerable strategy to implement.

To support this assertion, a host of evidence is made clear by the historical and contemporaneous practices of inequality, discrimination, and extinction occurring within this system of living. Examples of human life considered to have little or no value are aplenty—mass killings of children and adults across this nation due to gun violence, hate crimes, restricting a woman's reproductive rights, gender and racial income disparities, racial injustice, lack of equal access to medication in response to a pandemic, drug and alcohol addictions, increase in mental disorders, healthcare disparities, hunger and food calamities, homelessness, restricting voting rights of Black and Brown Americans, and a border refugee catastrophe. On June 15, 2022, Megan Brenan and Nicole Willcoxon published the results of a Gallup poll regarding American perception of moral values. The report states:

> A record-high 50 percent of Americans rate the overall state of moral values in the US as 'poor,' and another 37 percent say it is 'only fair.' Just 1 percent think the state of moral values 'excellent' and 12 percent 'good.' Although negative views of the nation's moral values have been the norm throughout Gallup's twenty-year trend, the current poor rating is the highest on record by one percentage point. Not only are Americans feeling grim about the current state of moral values in the nation, but they are also mostly pessimistic about the future on the subject, as 78 percent say morals are getting worse and just 18 percent getting better. The latest percentage saying moral values are getting worse is roughly in line with the average of 74 percent

since 2002, but it is well above the past two years' 67 percent and 68 percent readings. To better understand where Americans see problems with moral values, Gallop asked respondents to name the most important problem with the state of moral values in the US.

The most common response does not touch on any issue that has been the subject of public debate or social policy legislation in recent years, but rather on a more fundamental aspect of the way people treat each other. More Americans cite consideration of others (18 percent) than any other issue, as was the case when Gallop previously asked this question ten years ago. Beyond consideration of others, racism, lack of faith/religion, lack of morals, sense of entitlement and lack of a family structure are mentioned by 5 percent to 8 percent of US adults. Racism was less commonly mentioned in 2012 than it is now. The current state of moral values are the worst they have ever been. A lack of consideration for others is cited as the top problem, but racism has crept up as an issue.[54]

What Sherlock Holmes convincingly established was how the answer to any mystery is always discovered in the beginning if an individual is willing to reason backwards. The ability to reason backwards, commencing with the beginning of American history, provides an opportunity to understand an important yet mystifying

---

[54] Megan Brenan and Nicole Willcoxon, "Record-High 50 Percent of Americans Rate US Moral Values as 'Poor,'" *Gallup*, June 15, 2022, https://news.gallup.com /poll/393659/record-high-americans-rate-moral-values-poor.aspx.

predicament. The baffling dilemma has to do with how America's formal and impressive ceremonies celebrating a way of life as the "land of the free" with "liberty and justice for all" has fallen short of its pitched image. The American way of life has failed to be a forthright source of inspiration and encouragement for the development of moral authority amongst its populace. Professing to have achieved an illusion that this nation represents the "land of the free" with "liberty and justice for all" is nothing short of delusional.

On the contrary, tribalism, rather than community, has evolved within this nation to an alarming level where hate, bitterness, hostility, contempt, and immorality characterize a lack of tolerance, credibility, and relevance for anyone outside one's tribe. Americans have become one another's enemy when difference shows up within the territorial landscape. The path to counter tribalism with community requires an appreciation for human life as revealed through the recognition and value of individual inherent credibility that will nullify the ill effects of impoverishment. This will bring life to the words of the American astronomer, planetary scientist, cosmologist, astrophysicist, astrobiologist, author, and science communicator, Carl Edward Sagan: "In all our searching, the only thing we've found that makes the emptiness bearable is each other."[55]

Every now and then, it becomes imperative to draw upon the wisdom previously spoken by astute individuals from the past with an intention to correct a lack of discretion in the present times. One such individual is Frederick Douglass (1818–1895), an African American who escaped from slavery in Maryland and later rose to prominence in the nineteenth century as a social reformer, abolitionist, orator, writer, and statesman. Later into young adulthood, Douglass became a national leader of the abolitionist movement in Massachusetts and

---

[55] Carl Sagan, *Contact* (New York: Simon and Schuster, 1985).

New York. He gained more admiration in this nation and abroad for his powerful speeches and penetrating antislavery writings. Early into this nation's history, Frederick Douglass offered the American people a solution to reverse its system of living that fostered the idea human life for the powerless and oppressed was considered to have little or no value. During a speech to commemorate the twenty-third anniversary of the 1826 Emancipation Act in Washington, DC, which freed enslaved people in America's capital, Douglass stated: "The life of the nation is secure only while the nation is honest, truthful, and virtuous."[56]

After numerous failed attempts, Frederick Douglass, at the age of twenty, escaped from chattel slavery and fled to New York City on September 4, 1838. Douglass was only fourteen years old when in 1832, the senator, lawyer, politician, and judge from New York, William Learned Marcy, passionately defended his colleague, the ninth governor of New York, Martin Van Buren. His feverish rhetoric was to blatantly support Van Buren's right to receive President Andrew Jackson's nomination to the position of minister to Great Britain. This nomination by Jackson was to exert his political patronage, and Marcy also defended the president's right to wield this authority. Senator Henry Clay, who represented Kentucky, had just been defeated by Jackson in the 1832 presidential election. Clay harshly denounced this nomination as nothing more than the same patronage practices that had been practiced for years in Van Buren's home state of New York. It is easy to conclude from Henry Clay's reactionary posture he was seeking retaliation for having been attacked eight years earlier as a recipient of political patronage.[57]

---

[56] Frederick Douglass, "Address by Frederick Douglass" (Congregational Church, Washington, DC, April 16, 1883), https://www.loc.gov/resource/lcrbmrp.t0a04/?sp=4&r=-0.498,0.359,1.903,0.876,0.

[57] "The 1824 Election and the 'Corrupt Bargain,'" *USHistory.org*, accessed March 2, 2023, https://www.ushistory.org/us/23d.asp.

New York Senator William L. Marcy endorsed the appointment with a fabled and notorious statement that would later become attached to his political reputation. On January 25, 1832, while in the Senate, Marcy stated:

> It may be, sir, that the politicians of the United States are not so fastidious as some gentlemen are, as to disclosing the principles on which they act. They boldly preach what they practice. When they are contending for victory, they avow their intention of enjoying the fruits of it. If they are defeated, they expect to retire from the office. If they are successful, they claim, as a matter of right, the advantages of success. They see nothing wrong in the rule, that to the victor belong the spoils of the enemy.[58]

At the age of fourteen, Frederick Douglass had already learned the harsh reality associated with William Marcy's passionate declaration on the Senate floor: "They see nothing wrong in the rule, that to the victor belong the spoils of the enemy." Though the formulation of Marcy's words was new to the intellect inside the political arena, what Douglass had learned firsthand was that he was considered a human spoil by victors who saw nothing wrong with the rule of oppression: he was a chattel slave. As Frederick Douglass grew in his development as an educated man, there is no doubt that he came to understand the disturbing and harmful meaning attached; "to the victor belong the spoils of the enemy" had been in existence with the commencement of humankind.

---

[58] William Learned Marcy, "Remarks in the Senate" (Washington, DC, January 25, 1832), *Register of Debates in Congress, vol. 8, col. 1325, Bartleby,* https://www.bartleby.com/73/1314.html.

What Douglass learned at fourteen years of age was that women unattached to power, the poor, the uneducated, and BIPOC Americans were also considered human spoils by victors who supported a system of living based on the acquisition of power, authority, and domination. He learned at an early age that these same victors saw nothing wrong with the rule of oppression and the collection of human spoils. What Douglass did not know or envision was this list of Americans considered potential threats and, therefore, enemies to this system would increasingly grow throughout the development of this nation.

Over the ensuing decades, the list would grow to include the Asian, elderly, disabled, gay, lesbian, transgender, and immigrants exposed to this ideology of "to the victor belong the spoils of the enemy." The importance of examining this ideology, and its harmful impact upon American society, cannot be overstated. A system deficient in instituting a steadfast curriculum to educate an individual to recognize, value, and practice the traits expressive of principled character ignores the importance of an individual creating their personal moral blueprint. A system deficient in instituting this curriculum cannot live up to the principle: "The life of the nation is secure only while the nation is honest, truthful, and virtuous." Instead, tribalism, rather than community, will evolve with hate, bitterness, hostility, contempt, and immorality, characterizing the motivation to demean credibility, relevance, and value for anyone outside one's tribe. A way of life dominates where Americans become one another's enemy when difference shows up within the territorial landscape.

As previously stated, to ignore the establishing of a moral blueprint that runs parallel in importance to the cultural training and encouragement to value *what* a person is externally—be it gender, economic status, prominence, race, ethnicity, religion, physical appeal, or sexual orientation—initiates the personal need to pursue power, authority, and dominance. The pathway to achieve credibility and relevance in this manner inspires an individual to accept the false narrative that personal meaning and purpose are derived from external and material sources. If the goal in a person's life is to settle for mediocre and merely accept the limited and unstable legitimacy afforded to *what* an individual is, as derived from external and material sources, misfortune awaits.

The tragedy that arises from this decision is an inability to develop character based on principle and its equivalent of a moral blueprint. With the omission of both, an individual has only one criterion to develop their self-perception. The lone benchmarks to develop self-perception are by personal experiences that are either good, bad, or indifferent. A moral blueprint provides an individual with the opportunity to avoid internalizing experiences on emotional, psychological, and spiritual levels. The ability to separate from internalizing experiences is due to having developed a cache of personal qualities that comprise a person's intrinsic value and *who* that person is inherently.

Lacking a moral blueprint that provides information to confirm a person's authentic legitimacy, autonomy, and individuality to balance experiences that strictly focus on *what* an individual is makes it easy to develop a less-than-accurate self-perception. Therefore, for this moral blueprint deficiency, the need arises to create practices of inequality, discrimination, injustice, and extermination because an individual views their opportunities for success as limited. The advantage principled character provides an individual is a moral blueprint that identifies infinite opportunities for success due to possessing qualities that are distinct, excellent, and worthy.

A system of living that is negligent in providing an education to recognize, value, and practice innate qualities that exemplify admirable character still expects a person to demonstrate worthy character within that system one way or another. The threat of disregarding a societal law and the penalty of being incarcerated—rather than receiving encouragement and education to practice the qualities demonstrative of worthy character that represent a law of principle—locks in one expected outcome. Intellectual, emotional, and spiritual impoverishment will never be deterred from resurrecting old and creating new practices of inequality, discrimination, cruelty, and injustice that, in turn, take center stage within this system of living. The successful attainment of power, authority, and dominance based on value pertaining to *what* a person is externally and possesses materially is all that matters. Hence, "to the victor belong the spoils." The absence of promoting the education of personal autonomy, individuality, and innate intelligence through character development paves the way for this nation to revoke the words of Frederick Douglass: "The life of the nation is secure only while the nation is honest, truthful, and virtuous."

Again, to understand the origin as to why this nation is willing to revoke the words of Frederick Douglass, it becomes necessary to bring forth the words of Sherlock Holmes: "My dear friend Watson, in solving a problem of this sort, the grand thing is to be able to reason backwards. That is a very useful accomplishment, and a very easy one, but people do not practice it much." America's Founding Fathers mistakenly believed they could find a sustainable economic, political, and social shelter inside a democracy that was solely crafted to accommodate the group and their colleagues. The Founding Fathers and their colleagues were mostly educated men with law degrees, landowners, politicians, slave owners, and commerce entrepreneurs. On the whole, credibility, relevance, and value achieved by the Founding Fathers and their colleagues were predominantly based on a rationale of "the end justified the means."

The power, authority, and prominence this group of men amassed was protected by a Declaration of Independence initially designed to benefit the Founding Fathers and their colleagues. The statement, "We hold these truths to be self-evident, that all men are created equal, that they are endowed by their Creator with certain unalienable rights, that among these are life, liberty and the pursuit of happiness"[59] simply did not include any individual or group outside of the elite wealthy and powerful. Though the white male accounted for most of the wealth and power, there existed a much smaller group of Black and Indigenous males who attained lesser degrees of wealth and power. Emulating their white counterparts, wealth and power was achieved through ownership of slaves and land.

Professor Barbara Krauthamer, a distinguished historian regarding the subjects of this nation's slavery and emancipation during the nineteenth century, is credited with revealing the overlooked history of Native American slaveholders and the Black people they enslaved. Through her book titled *Black Slaves, Indian Masters: Slavery, Emancipation, and Citizenship in the Native American South*, Krauthamer discloses:

> From the late eighteenth century through the end of the Civil War, Choctaw and Chickasaw Indians bought, sold, and owned Africans and African Americans as slaves, a fact that persisted after the tribes' removal from the Deep South to Indian Territory. The tribes formulated racial and gender ideologies that justified this practice and marginalized free Black people in the Indian nations well after the Civil War and slavery had ended. Through the end

---

59 Thomas Jefferson, et al, "Declaration of Independence," July 4, 1776, *Library of Congress Archives*, https://www.loc.gov/item/mtjbib000159/.

of the nineteenth century, ongoing conflicts among Choctaw, Chickasaw, and US lawmakers left untold numbers of former slaves and their descendants in the two Indian nations without citizenship in either the Indian nations or the United States.[60]

At one time, recognized as one of the internet's top ten sites and founded in 2009, the *Listverse Newspaper* published an article on June 6, 2017, titled "Top Ten Black Slaveowners" by Aubrey Henderson, a graduate of Francis Marion University with a BA in English, and fact-checked by the paper's founder and head editor, Jamie Frater. Imitating their white counterparts to attain wealth and power, Anthony Johnson, William (April) Ellison, Antoine Dubuclet, Widow C. Richards and Son P.C. Richards, the Pendarvis Family, Marie Therese Metoyer, Dilsey Pope, Jacob Gasken, Nat Butler, Justus Angel, and Mistress L. Horry participated in a practice from the seventeenth thru the nineteenth centuries that basically safeguarded a one-dimensional ideology. This one-dimensional ideology that still remains in place during the modern era is one that recognizes the acquisition and execution of power, authority, and dominance over another fellow American is appropriate.[61]

The disturbing component is the appropriateness to implement this ideology no matter the cost to the "life, liberty, and the pursuit of happiness" to another credible and relevant human being. During this nation's beginning and contemporaneous times, the justification to restrict certain factions of Americans from being

---

[60] Barbara Krauthamer, *Black Slaves, Indian Masters: Slavery, Emancipation, and Citizenship in the Native American South* (US: University of North Carolina Press, 2013).

[61] Aubrey Henderson, "Top Ten Black Slaveowners," *Listverse*, June 6, 2017, https://listverse.com/2017/06/06/top-10-black-slaveowners/.

equal participants in voting rights, economic opportunities, and social issues by its power brokers is the price to pay for living in an unequal and inequitable America. The path to "life, liberty, and the pursuit of happiness" will come with limitations and discouragement for factions of people unable to satisfy what the system assesses as value. Living within a system that principally recognizes personal value based on the status regarding *what* an individual is externally and possesses materially is best overcome with a change of ideology. Develop "life, liberty, and the pursuit of happiness" based on the recognition of one's own intrinsic value, autonomy, and individuality that knows no such consequences as limitations and discouragement.

The eventual was sure to arrive when the wealthy and brokers of power assumed total responsivity for shifting economic, political, and social supremacy in their favor, which included stripping the Black and Indigenous of their resources to achieve wealth and power. The conception that all Americans were entitled to experience their indisputable rights to "life, liberty, and the pursuit of happiness" was considered an outlandish proposition during America's beginning. That same conception remains in the hearts and minds of some factions within American today. In this nation's beginning, the motivation for the affluent and elite to restrict "life, liberty, and the pursuit of happiness" in the form of voting rights for women, the BIPOC population, people who could not speak English, and residents between the ages of eighteen and twenty-one was motivated by fear of retribution. The fear revolved around the idea that if all Americans were granted the right of suffrage and equality—those who were not landowners and wealthy in comparison to the elite—these same factions could eventually rebel and usurp the wealth and land of the power brokers.

What follows in the next and final chapter eight are the conclusions resulting from the prophetic words of Sherlock Holmes. In addressing America's incapacity to be a nation of inspiration to all its inhabitants and other nations demonstrative of characteristics that define core values, such as being honest, truthful, and virtuous, "the grand thing is to be able to reason backwards. That is a very useful accomplishment, and a very easy one, but people do not practice it much."

Reasoning backwards to understand how yesterday's lack of a moral blueprint has become today's model for impoverishment reveals a nation wedded to power as a substitute for personal empowerment. The Founding Fathers utterly lacked an understanding regarding the importance of implementing an educational curriculum for an inexperienced nation that would help individuals recognize, value, and practice the best inherent qualities they bring into this existence. It is this type of learning that also provides individuals with the personal knowledge, skills, and perspective necessary to navigate and contribute to society regarding being just and equitable.

The Founding Fathers totally believed that the principles of liberty, equality, and self-government were sufficient to create a just and equitable society. The leaders of this young nation failed to recognize the role education and development of an individual's inherent credibility would play in diminishing issues of impoverishment reflected in the practices of discrimination, hatred, injustice, and corruption. Just as important, this education would play a key role in helping Americans to understand and appreciate the diversity of perspectives, experiences, and ideas that make up society, as well as contribute to that society.

Lastly, this education and personal development would be essential for individuals to understand the impact of their own biases, prejudices, and discrimination upon others that often leads to perpetuating inequality, hatred, injustice, and corruption. Personal development, self-awareness and critical thinking skills are fundamental to recognizing and challenging one's own biases and prejudices and to promoting greater understanding, empathy, and respect for others.

Chapter 8

FOUNDING FATHERS VS. EMPOWERED LEADERS

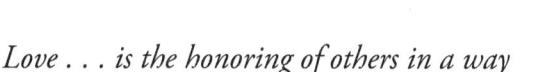

Love . . . is the honoring of others in a way
that grants them the grace of their own autonomy.
—Anne Truitt

You will face many defeats in life,
but never let yourself be defeated.
—Maya Angelou

A review of American history from its beginning to this current time period reveals a failure by Americans to coalesce and demonstrate amongst one another a moral blueprint that illustrates the theoretic words, "life, liberty, and the pursuit of happiness," expressed in its founding documents. As a result of this failure, the American community can be described as a fragmented society composed of a collection of interest groups—including, for example, the National Rifle Association (NRA) vs. Brady Campaign to Prevent Gun Violence, Planned Parenthood vs. National Right to Life Committee (NRLC), National Association for the Advancement of Colored People (NAACP) vs. Americans for Prosperity, American Civil

Liberties Union (ACLU) vs. Family Research Council (FRC), and the American Petroleum Institute (API) vs. Sierra Club.

For generations, the groups have been firmly alienated from one another along the lines of class, gender, race, ethnicity, politics, religion, and education. In recent years, however, this alienation has been consumed with the amplified presence of hatred, hostility, and cruelty. Differences and disagreements are inflamed by destitute intentions to discredit and destroy one another through methods of brutality, assault, and murder. We witness civilians, politicians, educators, and law enforcement helping to intensify a deeply fragmented society daily.

To establish a moral blueprint that represents a steadfast determination to give meaning to "every individual is entitled to life, liberty, and the pursuit of happiness" is out of the question. Living within a system that equates credibility, relevance, and value with the attainment of power, authority, and prominence effectively sets as rivals one American against another in a hostile and cruel manner. Rather than commit to assisting every American to be the best that person can be through the development of inherent qualities representative of substantive character, this society continues to nurture and groom intellectual, emotional, and spiritual impoverishment. Achieving equality and equity for every American, regardless of class, gender, race, ethnicity, education, age, politics, and religion, is viewed as a threat to the example set forth at the beginning of American history.

This should not come as a surprise to anyone who has studied American history. When this nation's original design was crafted by the Founding Fathers, their intent was to divide Americans along the lines of class, gender, race, ethnicity, education, age, politics, and religion. Equality and equity were meant for a certain segment of the populace. What is also no surprise was the common knowledge that the Founding Fathers—and many of their contemporaries—held personal views that were discriminatory toward the poor, racist toward the BIPOC populace, sexist toward women, and intolerant toward groups of people who could not speak English. Initially, the perpetrators of this behavior were mainly white males who were landowners, educated, and wealthy.

What is also known about the Founding Fathers and their colleagues is the fact that these elite men were products of their time and culture. They embraced racist, sexist, cruel, and discriminatory biases and prejudices that were considered to be normal and acceptable. With that said, this concocted rationalization cannot be accepted as justification to explain their unsavory behavior. Just as unacceptable is petitioning the same rationalization to explain the identical impoverished racist, sexist, cruel, and discriminatory biases and prejudices on display during the modern era. The act of breaking free from mainly the motherland, England, was primarily motivated due to living within a system dominated by discriminatory practices that were punitive and oppressive. Even so, these same English immigrants established practices in America that were also punitive and oppressive to people who were different from themselves. Once more, the oppressed became the oppressors upon reaching the shores of the new land.

Outside of their professional and wealthy lifestyles, the personal composition of the Founding Fathers, their contemporaries, and devoted followers is revealing. These powerful men, on a personal level, lacked individual meritorious character development, self-awareness, and critical thinking skills. During the days of American slavery, this white-male-dominated fraternity supported and contributed to the inhumane treatment of Black people held in bondage against their will. This sordid and immoral behavior became noticeable and prominent when Thomas Jefferson fathered six children with one of his female slaves, Sally Hemings. Of the six children, only Beverly, Harriet, Madison, and Eston Hemings survived to adulthood.

Adding insult to injury, this lack of meritorious character, his own self-awareness, and critical thinking created a vastly unbalanced relationship between Jefferson and Hemings. Hemings was a slave denied her basic rights and lived under constant exploitation and oppression. A number of men of Jefferson's era, including this Founding Father, established a new normal that continues to be in existence during this modern era. In many instances throughout the global community, women, much like Hemings, either have no basic rights, limited rights, or are viewed as the property of men.

Had these attributes been developed on a personal basis and practiced, these individuals would have been empowered to demonstrate the opposite of impoverishment toward groups of people outside of their culture. They would have been able to recognize and challenge their own biases and prejudices and promote greater understanding, empathy, and respect for all Americans rather than just a select few. This form of empowerment would have been a brilliant example to establish for the poor, women, the BIPOC populace, and people who could not speak English. Had this brand of credibility and relevance been established by the Founding Fathers, there would not have been any need on January 6, 2021, for more than 2,000 rioters to attack the United States Capitol in pursuit of what they were taught generations ago was their privilege and entitlement to retain: superiority.

Had this brand of credibility and relevance been established by the Founding Fathers, there would not have been a need for Americans during this nation's ensuing growth to become practitioners of oppression. Factions of white Americans comprising non-landowners, women, the poor, and the uneducated became perpetrators of discrimination, racism, gender inequality, and intolerance toward people who were not American. Though white women were being denied equal pay, access to healthcare as men, the right to vote, career choices, and education opportunities, there existed a faction exhibiting symptomatic behavior of intellectual, emotional, and spiritual impoverishment.

The list of perpetrators continued to grow and has expanded during the modern era to include women in support of gender inequality, different races, ethnicities, uneducated and poor exerting discrimination, and practices of injustice against their own group. Again, within a system of living where credibility and relevance are linked to the attainment of power, authority, and prominence, explicit and internalized tyranny is considered valid behavior to use against another person or group to reach the goal. Practitioners of internalized tyranny represent examples of how easy it is for the oppressed to become the oppressor. This is expressly true when lacking the education to acquire admirable character through the recognition and development of inherent qualities representative of a person's virtue.

There are two different but valid viewpoints when it comes to deciding the principal cause for a civilization's collapse: 1) a steady decline in moral values and 2) the influence of external factors, such as economic and political instabilities, environmental issues, repletion of resources, and external conflicts. The first point of view asserts that a steady decline in upholding moral values is the initial influence that generates the eventual collapse. Moral values are the doctrines and personal beliefs an individual espouses as good and bad, right and wrong, just and unjust.

Moral values such as honesty, integrity, fairness, humility, respect, responsibility, and forgiveness endorse human dignity for every individual within the community. As previously stated, an educational curriculum would help an individual recognize, value, and practice the best inherent qualities they bring into this existence. This same educational curriculum would help Americans to understand and appreciate the diversity of perspectives, experiences, and ideas that make up society and contribute to society. Adhering to moral values such as empathy, sincerity, concern for others, and recognizing one's own limitations and imperfections can become more than a theoretical exercise.

Two examples of moral values are located in this nation's founding documents—with one needing the written inclusion of women—but these have yet to be advanced beyond theoretical statements to an appreciable reality.

> Declaration of Independence: "We hold these truths to be self-evident, that all men (and women) are created equal, that they are endowed by their Creator with certain unalienable rights, that among these are life, liberty, and the pursuit of happiness."[62]

> The Constitution of the United States: "We the People of the United States, in Order to form a more perfect Union, establish Justice, ensure domestic Tranquility, provide for the common defense, promote the general welfare, and secure the Blessings of Liberty to ourselves and our Posterity, do ordain and establish this Constitution for the United States of America."[63]

---

[62] Declaration of Independence, *National Archives*, https://www.archives.gov/founding-docs/declaration-transcript.

[63] The United States Constitution, *National Archives*, https://www.archives.gov/founding-docs/constitution?_ga=2.37052576.1442457960.1681910415-1619124275.1681910415.

From this nation's beginning to the current era, the above-mentioned examples of moral values have yet to be an agreed-upon covenant by all Americans to advance to an appreciable reality. As a consequence, factions of the populace resist upholding the aforesaid moral values as standards that empower all Americans to experience "certain unalienable rights, that among these are life, liberty, and the pursuit of happiness." For many Americans, moral values have become extinct forms of confirmation so far as personal interactions are concerned. This is especially true when interactions intersect with different principles and viewpoints.

As moral values deteriorate, social fragmentation replaces cohesion with self-indulgence and self-importance. These two forms of impoverishment are unmasked through crime, corruption, cruelty, and addiction—which, if not impeded, can, in due course, lead to the collapse of a civilization. As a matter of fact, when these two forms of impoverishment are not impeded, the collapse of a culture, marriage, family, or relationship becomes inevitable.

The landscape of American authority figures is besieged with leaders from all sectors of the nation. In spite of this saturation, leadership skills are dreadfully lacking with respect to marshaling a compelling commitment to save this nation from self-destruction. No matter what side of the difference—Democrat or Republican, liberal or conservative, pro-life or pro-choice, right to bear arms or gun control, working class or affluent, anti-systemic racism and discrimination activists or advocates for racial disparities being non-existent—the objectives for both sides are rather clear.

The Founding Fathers did not leave subsequent generations of the populace with righteous examples where the welfare of this nation took precedence over personal interest. Today's objective with handling differences is consistent with the Founding Fathers' intention of attaining power, authority, and prominence. Protecting personal interest, rather than this nation's welfare, was an example launched early at the beginning of this nation. Julie Zauzmer Weil, Adrián Blanco Ramos, and Leo Dominguez aptly capture that investment in a *Washington Post* exclusive report on January 10, 2022, under the caption: "More than 1,800 congressmen once enslaved Black people. This is who they were and how they shaped the nation."

> The *Washington Post* has compiled the first database of slaveholding members of Congress by examining thousands of pages of census records and historical documents. From the founding of the United States until long after the Civil War, hundreds of the elected leaders writing the nation's laws were current or former slave owners. More than 1,800 people who served in the US Congress in the eighteenth, nineteenth, and even twentieth centuries owned human beings at some point in their lives.[64]

There is no genuine investment in generating amicable discussions to resolve underlying causes that divide and fragment this nation's populace. Instead, the emphasis for both sides of the discussions is directed at dramatizing the lackluster effort to solve symptoms rather than an honest endeavor to address a basic societal problem. Inequity, inequality, deceit, greed, racism, discrimination, hatred, mass killings, and the presence of more guns than citizens represent symptoms that materialize due to a moral disorder. Historically, this

---

[64] Julie Zauzmer Weil, et al, "More Than 1,800 Congressmen Once Enslaved Black People. This Is Who They Were, and How They Shaped the Nation," *The Washington Post*, January 10, 2022, https://www.washingtonpost.com/history/interactive/2022/congress-slaveowners-names-list/

type of disorder has dominated life in America as evidenced by an indifference to the suffering of another person or group that results from the aforementioned symptoms. This disorder has made it nearly impossible for the moral values expressed throughout the Declaration of Independence and the Constitution of the United States to be embraced as a practical blueprint to champion.

As long as this nation lacks a social course of study focusing on the recognition of inherent credibility that comprises attributes symbolic of substantive character, the focus of the discussions on differences will remain with an investment in being right. With a focus linked to this type of investment, the end goal is attaining power, authority, and prominence over a faction representing the difference. Rather than leaders partaking in virtuous and principled discussions to resolve the genuine societal problem of intellectual, emotional, and spiritual impoverishment, deflection and avoidance protects their actual agenda.

The objective of creating a dedicated social course of study is to give all Americans an opportunity to reverse the moral disorder. Achieving perfection is not part of this strategy, for there will always be individuals who will choose to settle for the pursuit of power, authority, and prominence. Rather than step out from the obscurity of mediocrity to accept the responsibility for one's autonomy, empowerment, and wisdom, it is much easier to remain unaware, indifferent, and impoverished regarding the gifts of character.

As previously stated in Chapter 7, the role of an education and development pertaining to an individual's inherent credibility would play a huge role in diminishing issues of impoverishment reflected in the practices of hatred, discrimination, injustice, and corruption. This education would also play a key role in helping Americans to understand and appreciate the diversity of perspectives, experiences, and ideas that make up society, as well as to contribute to this society. This education and personal development would be essential for individuals to understand the impact of their own biases, prejudices, and discrimination upon others that often lead to perpetuating inequality, hatred, injustice, and corruption. Personal development, self-awareness and critical thinking skills are fundamental to recognizing and challenging one's own biases and prejudices and to promoting greater understanding, empathy, and respect for others.

The second point of view with respect to causes for the collapse of civilizations, alluded to earlier in the chapter, has to do with how economic and political instabilities, environmental decay, resource depletion, climate change, internal clashes, and external conflicts can be substantial factors to consider. The opinion that an external intrusion can cause a civilization—as well as a culture, marriage, or family—to collapse without an internal breach first occurring remains a topic of discussion to debate. There is no question—external intrusions such as earthquakes, hurricanes, economic downturns, corruption, criminal activity, marital divorce, and family separation can have a negative impact upon a community. However, where there exists a cohesive community fundamentally structured around the practice of moral values united to protect, preserve human life, and respect the dignity of every individual within a community, the end result is clear. The incursion may claim its material spoils. With that being said, the intrusion will never claim the spirit and soul of the community, which guarantees against the possibility of total collapse.

As also stated in Chapter 7, world history is crammed with numerous civilizations and empires that have collapsed due to various external sources. It is important to mention that history also reveals three civilizations that emphasized among their populaces the importance of demonstrating ideals such as honesty, integrity, responsibility, and respect for human life and dignity. The ancient Greek democracy, Islamic Golden Age, and the Renaissance are credited by historians with emphasizing the importance of practicing honorable attributes of character. All three civilizations experienced more prosperity than many civilizations that did not emphasize and practice similar standards.

However, a common thread that subsequently surfaced for each of the three was that they were eventually overtaken by another civilization. A society lacking a moral blueprint that is reflective of inherent credibility to equal importance as bestowed upon prosperity will reveal a susceptibility to power, authority, and prominence. Moral values that translate into a common theme united to protect and preserve human life, as well as the dignity of every individual within the community, will avoid the susceptibility to being overtaken by self-importance and self-indulgence.

The first civilization to emphasize among its populace the importance of demonstrating ideals with respect for human life and dignity was the ancient Greek democracy.

> "In a democracy," the Greek historian Herodotus wrote, "there is, first, that most splendid of virtues, equality before the law." It was true that the Athenian lawgiver, Cleisthenes (c.570–c.508 BC), is credited with reforming the constitution of ancient Athens and setting it on a democratic footing in 508 BC. His *demokratia* abolished the political distinctions between the Athenian aristocrats who had long monopolized the political decision-making process and the middle-and working-class people who made up the army and the navy (and whose incipient discontent was the reason Cleisthenes introduced his reforms in the first place).

However, around 460 BC, under the rule of the general Pericles (generals were among the only public officials who were elected, not appointed), Athenian democracy began to evolve into something that we would call an aristocracy: the rule of what Herodotus called "the one man, the best." Though democratic ideals and processes did not survive in ancient Greece, they have been influencing politicians and governments ever since.[65]

The second civilization to emphasize among its populace the importance of demonstrating ideals with respect for human life and dignity was the Islamic Golden Age.

For centuries, the city of Timbuktu, located in the center of present-day Mali in Western Africa, thrived as one of the bustling centers of culture and learning during the Golden Age of Islam. The region's legacy as an intellectual destination begins with the Epic of Sundiata. According to the thirteenth-century epic poem, the Mandinka prince of the Kangaba state organized a successful resistance against the harsh Sosso King Sumaoro Kanté—and a new empire was born. Under Mansa Musa I and his successors, Timbuktu transformed from a small but successful trading post into a center of commerce and scholarship, making the Mali Empire one of the most influential of the Golden Age of Islam. Powerful West African kings and Islamic leaders traveled from far and wide to Timbuktu to trade, learn, and foster strong political allies.

---

[65] "Ancient Greek Democracy," *History.com*, August 19, 2019, https://www.history.com/topics/ancient-greece/ancient-greece-democracy.

Brent D. Singleton writes that "in Timbuktu, literacy and books transcended scholarly value and symbolized wealth, power, and baraka (blessings)" and that the acquisition of books specifically "is mentioned more often than any other display of wealth." By the sixteenth century, Timbuktu hosted 150 to 180 Qur'anic schools or Maktabs. Malian rulers also built great mosques, not only for spiritual practice but also as centers of learning of mathematics, law, grammar, history, geography, astronomy and astrology.

The Mali Empire declined in the fifteenth century and was replaced by the Songhai Empire. Askia Muhammad, a military leader from the Malian city of Gao, reigned from 1492 and 1528 and fortified the Islamic learning tradition in Timbuktu that his predecessors had set forth. But soon, Timbuktu found itself under threat when the Moroccan Saadian dynasty invaded the Songhai Empire in the late sixteenth century. Many of Timbuktu's centers of learning were destroyed, and many people's possessions, including important manuscripts, were lost. The Golden Age of Islamic scholarship, architecture, and culture in the Songhai Empire and across West Africa had seriously diminished.[66]

The third civilization to emphasize among its populace the importance of demonstrating ideals with respect for human life and dignity was the Italian Renaissance.

---

[66] Kai Mora, "How Timbuktu Flourished During the Golden Age of Islam," *History.com*, June 6, 2022, https://www.history.com/news/timbuktu-mali-africa-islam.

The Renaissance was a fervent period of European cultural, artistic, political, and economic "rebirth" following the Middle Ages. Generally described as taking place from the fourteenth century to the seventeenth century, the Renaissance promoted the rediscovery of classical philosophy, literature and art. Some of the greatest thinkers, authors, statesmen, scientists and artists in human history thrived during this era, while global exploration opened up new lands and cultures to European commerce. The Renaissance is credited with bridging the gap between the Middle Ages and modern-day civilization.

During the fourteenth century, a cultural movement called humanism began to gain momentum in Italy. Among its many principles, humanism promoted the idea that man was the center of his own universe and people should embrace human achievements in education, classical arts, literature, and science. In 1450, the invention of the Gutenberg printing press allowed for improved communication throughout Europe and for ideas to spread more quickly.

As a result of this advance in communication, little-known texts from early humanist authors such as those by Francesco Petrarch and Giovanni Boccaccio, which promoted the renewal of traditional Greek and Roman culture and values, were printed and distributed to the masses. As more people learned how to read, write and interpret ideas, they began to closely examine and critique religion as they knew it. Also, the printing press allowed for texts, including the Bible, to be easily reproduced and widely read by the people themselves for the first time.

Scholars believe the demise of the Renaissance was the result of several compounding factors. By the end of the fifteenth century, numerous wars had plagued the Italian peninsula. Spanish, French, and German invaders battling for Italian territories caused disruption and instability in the region. Also, changing trade routes led to a period of economic decline and limited the amount of money that wealthy contributors could spend on the arts.

Later, in a movement known as the Counter-Reformation, the Catholic church censored artists and writers in response to the Protestant Reformation. Many Renaissance thinkers feared being too bold, which stifled creativity. Furthermore, in 1545, the Council of Trent established the Roman Inquisition, which made humanism and any views that challenged the Catholic church an act of heresy punishable by death. By the early seventeenth century, the Renaissance movement had died out, giving way to the Age of Enlightenment.[67]

During this modern era, the Nordic countries—Denmark, Finland, Iceland, Norway, Sweden—as well as the Faroe Islands, Greenland, and Åland, are recognized by their assessments as excellent examples of prosperity and social advancement throughout the world. Paula Lehtomäki, the secretary general representing the

---

[67] "Renaissance," *History.com*, March 28, 2023, https://www.history.com/topics/renaissance/renaissance#:~:text=The%20Renaissance%20was%20a%20fervent,classical%20philosophy%2C%20literature%20and%20art.

Nordic Council of Ministers, comments in the preface of her State of the Nordic Region 2020 report:

> We ... are proud of many of the characteristics of our part of the world. We have low levels of inequality, balanced welfare provisions and dynamic, innovative and resilient economies. Our democracy and our welfare model are based on high levels of education and long-life expectancy, combined with substantial investments in research and innovation. Mobility and macroregional integration allow us to study, travel, work, and start businesses in each other's countries. The peaceful, democratic, and inclusive nature of our communities helps make our societies strong and resilient.
>
> We have frequently shown that the Nordic countries are stronger together. We learn from each other and share experiences to accumulate knowledge and highlight best practices. Sharing knowledge is also what crystallizes the main purpose of this report: to provide insights from local, regional, and national levels to the Nordic level, using infographics, maps, data and analyses.
>
> As a Nordic information package, this report is one of a kind. The socioeconomic trends studied in it are key indicators for all of us who work with development. It shows the results of our work and helps us detect where a shift in focus is needed. The twelve chapters constitute a basis for policy development in a diverse Nordic Region.[68]

---

[68] Paula Lehtomäki, "Preface," *State of the Nordic Region 2020*, March 2, 2020, https://pub.norden.org/nord2020-001/#78633.

The first nail in the coffin for a civilization spiraling downward toward collapse is a decline in the actual application or use of moral values. A depreciation regarding the practicality of principled behavior contributes to the creation of a disjointed society. The type of leadership required to help prevent this depreciation occurs when leaders position themselves to learn, value, and practice their inherent credibility. This becomes a transformative experience for the continuation of their personal character development. Attributes such as visionary thinking, strategic planning, adaptability, collaboration, and good communication skills become extensions of this development. The recognition of inherent credibility and character development are critical examples for people to follow that will help prevent societal fragmentation and initiate a united populace.

Perceptive leadership learns from these personal transformative experiences the importance of initiating a curriculum that educates a populace to identify, value, and practice inherent qualities that exemplify honorable character. To unify a society abundant with diversity requires this educational curriculum to help all of its inhabitants develop an appreciation for autonomy, individuality, self-awareness, and critical thinking skills. It is vastly important that inhabitants of a diverse society learn that each and every individual within the community shares with one another a profound common denominator. This shared similarity goes beyond the limits of credibility and relevance based on *what* an individual is externally and possesses materially. This common denominator represents personal legitimacy that is bestowed upon each individual based on substantive qualities that characterize inherent credibility.

This newly defined legitimacy ensures that everyone throughout the civilization experiences equality in terms of options and equity in terms of economic prosperity. Fair and just exchanges sustained by all-embracing moral values in a literal sense are history in the making rather than a historic abstraction. The true external factors, such as environmental natural disasters, climate change, misuse of internal resources, economic downfall, the erosion of a labor force, and political factors, such as corruption, and internal conflict, can contribute to a civilization's downfall. However, when there is an internal breakdown associated with an inability to practice ethical standards that honor all individuals within the community, the outcome is predictable and irrefutable. Moral disintegration and societal fragmentation precipitate the actual downfall.

History is crammed with examples regarding the collapse of civilizations, governments, and social, political, and religious institutions due to a person's inherent credibility being considered less significant than external credibility. The Roman, British, Japanese, Spanish, Russian, and Mongol Empires eventually collapsed primarily due to an inability to balance a way of life negatively impacted by immorality with moral doctrines. Placing the focus on recognizing and practicing inherent credibility initiates the development of substantive character. Whereas a principal focus on recognizing external credibility and relevance initiates the unsafe practices of betrayal and corruption. Any system of living, whether a collective or individual effort, that encourages power, authority, and dominance to sustain self-importance and self-indulgence establishes a state of intellectual, emotional, and spiritual impoverishment.

The Founding Fathers launched this nation onto its current path to represent American exceptionalism as distinctive and unique, primarily in terms of self-government, material resources, and individuality. However, our nation has reached a critical point in its evolution, as have many previous civilizations that failed to grasp the bigger picture regarding the importance of moral development.

It is time to break with our Founding Fathers' historical legacy that excluded exceptionalism, also being defined by the recognition of inherent credibility that comprises attributes symbolic of substantive character. This type of exceptionalism diminishes the presence of spiritual impoverishment and is truly historically distinctive and unique when compared to past and present civilizations.

Chapter 9

A HISTORICAL COMMONALITY SHARED

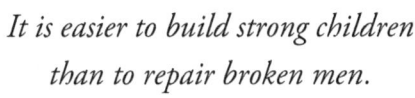

It is easier to build strong children
than to repair broken men.
—Frederick Douglass

I have great respect for the past.
If you don't know where you've come from,
you don't know where you're going.
I have respect for the past, but I'm a person of the moment.
I'm here, and I do my best to be completely
centered at the place I'm at,
then I go forward to the next place.
—Maya Angelou

Cecil Day-Lewis, the father of actor Sir Daniel Day-Lewis, was an Irish-born British poet laureate from 1968 until his death in 1972 and a writer of crime novels under the pen name of Nicholas Blake. As a celebrated poet and mystery writer, Cecil Day-Lewis is best known for his brilliant statement: "We do not write in order to be understood; we write in order to understand."

Impartial history is written to understand the advancements and failings of a society, which can shed light on the implementation of improvements to both classifications. Imploring Sherlock Holmes' statement that the answer to every mystery can be found in the beginning helps to reinforce Cecil Day-Lewis's statement of "we write in order to understand." Interlaced throughout both statements is a focus on understanding.

Writing to be understood enhances the probability of creating a biased transcription of history due to writing to please an audience. In contrast, writing with a focus on understanding enhances the opportunity to learn about the various methods used to bring about advancements and the reasons for the failings of a society. There is no question as to this country's status as one of the most advanced technological and industrial nations worldwide. Second to none are America's economic power, democratic system of government, scientific discoveries, and military power.

What also remains not in question, however, is the inability of America to develop and live by a moral blueprint that keeps pace with its scientific discoveries and industrial, technological, and military advancements. A lack of recognition regarding inherent credibility creates a less than enthusiastic social acceptance in comparison to the passionate and favorable social reception bestowed upon prosperity. America's internal weakness continues to be historically revealed because of this discrepancy. This nation's Achilles' heel is susceptibility to being intellectually, emotionally, and spiritually dominated by the incessant need to attain power, authority, and prominence in order to achieve a one-dimensional sense of credibility and relevance.

As discussed in Chapter 8, societies such as the ancient Greek democracy, Islamic Golden Age, and Renaissance lived through formidable levels of prosperity, as America has achieved. Over a period of time, however, each of the three civilizations eventually came to experience a collapse as formidable as their prosperous rise. History has exposed a general rule that has been proven to be valid and consistent: When society fails to establish an equal recognition for guidelines exemplifying moral values that equal the recognition and value of prosperity, intellectual, emotional, and spiritual impoverishment will prevail.

The community will be unable to avoid being overtaken by the self-importance and self-indulgence of another civilization due to a lack of internal cohesion. The same rule applies when cultural disintegration occurs due to a breakdown of shared values. Restricting equality in terms of options and equity in terms of economic prosperity is designed to deny another individual or group the opportunity to experience their credibility and relevance; this makes it impossible to remain as a cohesive community. Nonexistent is a pervasive and embracing theme that states people are united together to protect and preserve human life, which includes the dignity of every individual.

As also discussed in Chapter 8, the final nail in the coffin that precipitates a collapse is the dominance of moral decay that has deeply divided people. It is virtually impossible for a society, culture, or entity to remain a cohesive community when there is a deterioration in ethical and moral values, principles, and standards of behavior. The blatant presence of poverty, racism, gender inequality, polarization, increased crime rates, declining standards of education, erosion of family values, and an overall indifference toward social responsibility are classic examples of moral decay. The quality of life continues to be negatively impacted throughout this nation. Self-indulgence and self-importance, as exhibited through the rise of individualism, consumerism, and materialism, is evidence an additional form of education is needed to reach the populace throughout America.

The time to teach an individual to recognize, value, and practice meritorious qualities that represent their inherent credibility has arrived. The graveyard is crammed with ancient and modern fallen societies that were once overwhelmed with individualism, consumerism, and materialism prior to their collapse—the Sumerian Civilization, Roman Empire, Aztec Empire, Han dynasty, Byzantine Empire, Ottoman Empire, British Empire, and the Soviet Union. The lack of cohesion amongst the populace who comprise this nation—that was once based on a moral principle that every individual is entitled to "life, liberty, and the pursuit of happiness"—can be reversed. But before this reversal can take place, we must acknowledge how we as a nation arrived at this most crucial moment in our existence in order to break with a historical model.

The Constitutional rights website states:

> In February 1787, Congress decided that a convention should be convened to revise the Articles of Confederation, the nation's first Constitution. In May, 55 delegates came to Philadelphia, and the Constitutional Convention began. Debates erupted over-representation in Congress, over slavery, and over the new executive branch. The debates continued through four hot and muggy months. But eventually, the delegates reached compromises, and on September 17, they produced the US Constitution, replacing the Articles with the governing document that has functioned effectively for more than 200 years.[69]

However, before the September 17 date, James Madison, the fourth president of the United States, delivered a speech on August

---

[69] "The Founders and the Vote," *Library of Congress*, https://www.loc.gov/classroom-materials/elections/right-to-vote/the-founders-and-the-vote/.

7, 1787, in the Constitutional Convention on voting rights, titled, "Note to His Speech on the Right of Suffrage." Madison proclaimed:

> The right of suffrage is a fundamental Article in Republican constitutions. The regulation of it is, at the same time, a task of peculiar delicacy. Allow the right exclusively to property, and the rights of persons may be oppressed. The feudal polity alone sufficiently proves it. Extend it equally to all, and the rights of property or the claims of justice may be overruled by a majority without property or interested in measures of injustice.

> In a just and a free government, therefore, the rights both of property and of persons ought to be effectually guarded. Will the former be so in the case of a universal and equal suffrage? Will the latter be so in the case of a suffrage confined to the holders of property? As the holders of property have at stake all the other rights common to those without property, they may be the more restrained from infringing, as well as the less tempted to infringe the rights of the latter.

> It is nevertheless certain, that there are various ways in which the rich may oppress the poor; in which property may oppress liberty; and that the world is filled with examples. It is necessary that the poor should have a defense against the danger. On the other hand, the danger to the holders of property cannot be disguised, if they be undefended against a majority without property.[70]

---

[70] "James Madison, Note to His Speech on the Right of Suffrage," *University of Chicago Press*, https://press-pubs.uchicago.edu/founders/documents/v1ch16s26.html.

James Madison, one of the Founding Fathers of the United States, is known for his role in drafting the United States Constitution and the Bill of Rights. In theory, Madison believed in the principle of equal representation and advocated for the protection of minority rights, which included voting rights. In practice, however, Madison's views on voting rights were more complex and based on self-interest. He believed that property ownership was a prerequisite for responsible citizenship and that only property-owning men should have the right to vote. This view was based on the idea that property owners had a vested interest in the stability and prosperity of the nation. With this alleged vested interest, the wealthy and property owners were, therefore, more likely to make responsible economic, social, and political decisions. Again, complexity is heightened and enters the backdrop due to Madison's fear that if minorities were given voting rights, these same factions could eventually rebel and usurp the wealth and land of his contemporaries.

When the United States was solely an agricultural society during Madison's time and property ownership was viewed as a symbol of financial stability and independence, a precedence was established that has negatively impacted this nation throughout its existence. This preference given to the wealthy and property owners over other factions of the populace generated significant imbalances in terms of economic, social, and political policies, and it is true these same negative results remain a serious problem for this nation today. The preference for property owners has led to policies and laws that favor the wealthy and powerful over marginalized groups, which has contributed to issues of low wages, absurd CEO buyouts, gender inequality, racial discrimination, and unsafe employment conditions.

Problems of this nature continue to be major challenges that America must address today, and they are rooted in the historical and systemic inequalities that have been created by the preference for protecting property owners over factions of the populace. James Madison was unable to separate himself from a reality occurring from its beginning within an American system of living. That particular reality fostered the idea that outside the powerful and property owners, human life was considered to be of little importance. The words of Frederick Douglass, "The life of the nation is secure only while the nation is honest, truthful, and virtuous," would come to be a theoretical proposition.

From the Library of Congress:

> Eventually, the framers of the Constitution left details of voting to the states. Initially, states limited this right to property-owning or tax-paying white males (about 6 percent of the population). Unfortunately, leaving election control to individual states led to unfair voting practices in the US.
>
> At first, white men with property were the only Americans routinely permitted to vote. President Andrew Jackson, champion of frontiersmen, helped advance the political rights of those who did not own property. The 1828 presidential election was the first in which non-property-holding white males could vote in the vast majority of states. By the end of the 1820s, attitudes and state laws had shifted in favor of universal white male suffrage. By about 1860, most white men without property were enfranchised.[71]

Thomas Jefferson, the third president of the United States, was another Founding Father who helped to create a precedent that

---

[71] "The Founders and the Vote," *Library of Congress*, https://www.loc.gov/classroom-materials/elections/ right-to-vote/the-founders-and-the-vote/.

encircled American exceptionalism within the restraints of contradiction and ambiguity. It is true that Jefferson believed in the principles of freedom and democracy. It is also true, however, that his beliefs did not extend to all members of society at the time. He held personal views that were racist and sexist, which included that enslaved Africans, women, Native Americans, and other marginalized groups should not have the same rights and freedoms as white male citizens. Jefferson also believed that the ability to speak English was a prerequisite for full citizenship.

It is not surprising to learn that Jefferson's personal views were not unique to him and were commonly held by many of his contemporaries. It is important to recognize that Jefferson and Madison shared identical personal views regarding upholding the principles of inequality. These shared viewpoints included the lack of equal access to opportunities and resources for people who might otherwise be excluded or marginalized, and in fact, aligned with that of the nation during their contemporary times.

Robert Warren Tucker, a writer and teacher of American foreign policy at Johns Hopkins University, and David C. Hendrickson, a professor of political science at Colorado College and a member of the Coalition for a Realistic Foreign Policy, coauthored a book released in 1992 titled *Empire of Liberty: The Statecraft of Thomas Jefferson.* The authors capture Jefferson's contradiction and ambiguity quite well.

Tucker and Hendrickson state:

> Jefferson believed America's exceptionalism was the bearer of a new diplomacy, founded on the confidence of a free and virtuous people, that would secure ends based on the natural and universal rights of man, by means that escaped war and its corruptions.
>
> Jefferson envisaged America becoming the world's great Empire of Liberty, the model for democracy

and republicanism. He identified his nation as a beacon to the world, as he said when he departed the presidency in 1809. Trusted with the destinies of this solitary republic of the world, the only monument of human rights, and the sole depository of the sacred fire of freedom and self-government, from hence it is to be lighted up in other regions of the earth, if other areas of the earth shall ever become susceptible of its benign influence.[72]

The contradiction soon follows when Tucker and Hendrickson state:

The Empire of Liberty was to be made up of one people dedicated to liberty under republican institutions. There was to be no place here for subjects, only for citizens. This was why, in principle, Negroes could have no permanent position within the palladium of freedom and why, in practice, Indians (and women) as well had to be excluded from it.[73]

The grandiose thinking that captivated the Founding Fathers and their colleagues can be explained with one statement. The belief these men were creating an America that was unique and exceptional greatly inflated their personal sense of self-importance and self-indulgence. The big picture thought to be in the making was actually a miniature version of the old-world order of monarchy and aristocracy. Within the group were the wealthy, educated landowners, gender dominant, and slaveowners who held deeply ingrained

---

[72] Robert W. Tucker, et al, *Empire of Liberty: The Statecraft of* Thomas Jefferson (United Kingdom: Oxford University Press, 1992), ix.

[73] Tucker, *Empire*, 161.

racial prejudices. It was not unusual for individuals within this inner circle of influence to struggle to reconcile a commitment to liberty and equality with the reality of slavery and inequality in American society.

Jefferson's grandiose thinking literally shattered the opportunity for him to grasp the bigger picture regarding the concept of exceptionalism for America. He easily rationalized this nation coming into its existence with a special purpose that would serve as a model and a beacon of democracy and freedom to the world. Going outside the limits of acceptable judgment, however, Jefferson believed the principles of liberty, equality, and democracy that were the solid foundation of this nation's system were universal and timeless. Exceptionalism would have had an original and authentic meaning had women, the BIPOC populace, the Asian populace, the uneducated, and the poor been originally included in America's promise of "life, liberty, and the pursuit of happiness."

When a person is unaware of the attributes that exemplify their inherent credibility, it is difficult to recognize and value the legitimacy of another individual or group with different influences and life experiences. Due to this condition of impoverishment, attempting to grasp what exactly involves a bigger picture in relation to the legitimacy of a diversified community becomes an annoying undertaking. To further complicate the irksome task, lacking information pertaining to one's true value means the internal vacuum symbolizing a state of impoverishment is commonly revealed through acts of power, authority, and dominance with respect to relationships.

The inability to grasp the bigger picture in terms of maximizing challenges and endeavors when the outcome could benefit an immense number of people has been common throughout history. Self-interest—disclosed through acts that generate economic disparities, gender inequality, racism, ethnic cleansing, genocide, discrimination, and injustice—has one perverse purpose in mind. The agenda is to cripple the responsibility that comes attached to bringing forth a big-picture vision.

Again, it is difficult to be aware of one's full potential to achieve goals that are multilayered while lacking information pertaining to meritorious personal attributes that can assure a measure of success. Unfortunately, the Founding Fathers and their colleagues lacked this personal information, which impeded their ability to grasp America's bigger picture. The opportunity for all of America's populace to share in an original and far-reaching exceptionalism was lost due to their egocentric pledge to self-interest. This self-centered approach took precedence over the interest in creating an all-inclusive nation.

Eighty-nine years after the founding of America, another example of failing to understand the bigger picture would cost the celebrated General Robert E. Lee and the South a possible victory over the Union Army during this nation's Civil War. Alan Daniel, an author and former practicing attorney with a JD in Law from Pepperdine University School of Law in 1978, responds to the question, "What was Robert E. Lee's greatest weakness?"

> General William T. Sherman sent a letter to General Ulysses S. Grant during the Civil War as he was marching through Georgia identifying Lee's greatest weakness. He told Grant that now they (the Union side) would find out if Lee was a detail man or a big picture man. Sherman thought Lee failed as a "big picture" man who could see the overall strategic situation; rather, he was more of a tactician who was excellent at individual battles but not so good at the overall scheme.

> Sherman was correct, as Lee failed to respond to Sherman's devastating march through Georgia that

destroyed the will of the South to go on with the war and deprived them of food. Grant's taking of Richmond was terrible for the Confederates, but Sherman's march through their heartland and the destruction of their valuable food supplies was a killing blow, and that had already been landed when Richmond fell. In my opinion, Sherman correctly identified Lee's greatest weakness; he was a detail man.

Lee failed to see the importance of holding the harbors along the Atlantic coast, and the Confederates totally failed to properly defend their most important assets, such as New Orleans or Vicksburg. At both locations, they needed better outer defenses, more stockpiles of food, and mobile units to raid the Union supply lines after they had adopted a siege. Lee should have been able to impact all these decisions, but he did not because he focused so closely on his forces in Virginia. That is a detail man, as Sherman put it, and not a big picture man.[74]

Michael Hutton, a Georgetown University Graduate in 1987 with an MA in national security studies, adds this information to the Robert E. Lee profile. Hutton states:

Robert E. Lee was a battlefield commander. His critical failing, though, was his inability to understand how technology had changed the nature of war since Napoleon's armies had fought in Europe. Lee believed

---

[74] Alan Daniel, "What Was Robert E. Lee's Greatest Weakness?" *Quora*, https://www.quora.com/What-was-Robert-E-Lees-greatest-weakness.

deeply that frontal, tactical assaults would achieve decisive results, but he failed to understand that his tactics would lead to the destruction of the offensive power of his army and make him the commander who suffered more casualties than any other commander in the Civil War—Union or Confederate.

The Civil War and the beginning of modern warfare. Most historians consider the Civil War as the "first modern war due to an unprecedented mobilization of the civilian base in both the Union and the Confederacy" and because it was [characterized] by technological innovations that increased the ability of armies to inflict heavy casualties' orders of magnitude quicker than in wars past.

Confederate Army General Thomas "Stonewall" Jackson, Union Army Generals Ulysses S. Grant, George Thomas, and William T. Sherman understood this change. Lee did not. And he would make this fatal tactical error the foundation of his doctrine throughout the war, continuing to believe in the illusion that frontal assaults could achieve a decisive victory. Lee's greatest tactical errors.

As Porter Alexander, Lee's brilliant Confederate artilleryman, noted after the war in his memoirs: "Lee took a great risk for no chance of gain except the killing of some thousands of his enemy with the loss of, perhaps, two-thirds as many of his own men. That was a losing game for the Confederacy. Its supply of men was limited; that of the enemy was not. That was not war!"[75]

General Robert E. Lee is an important American historical person to study. The main reason is he exemplified on the battlefield the same lack of forethought as did the Southern culture he represented. Lee was simply a product of his culture. Together, the South and Lee committed tactical errors that contributed roughly to 258,000 Confederate deaths and hastened the inevitable. Withdrawal from the Union to form the Confederacy was undeniably not going to take place. The North had overwhelming finances, technological innovations, leadership, fighting force, supply lines, armaments, and Thomas Jefferson's legacy regarding American exceptionalism. The inability to envision the big historical picture on the part of the South and General Lee spelled certain defeat and the needless loss of men.

The Southern states engaged in the American Civil War between the years 1861 to 1865 for a number of reasons, which were to protect values that essentially intersected and coincided with one another. For example, the increase of federal power was viewed as a direct threat to the Southern states' way of life and economic interest. Slave labor was considered an essential component of the Southern states' production of their agricultural economy, which predominantly consisted of cotton and tobacco. There was great fear the Northern states would ultimately end slavery, which would create an economic downfall for the South and instigate unwelcome social and racial changes. Another fear was the Southern states' belief the industrialized Northern states would unfairly receive more economic recognition and benefits than the South's economy, primarily based on agriculture.

---

[75] Michael Hutton, "What Was Robert E. Lee's Greatest Weakness?" *Quora*, https://www.quora.com/What-was-Robert-E-Lees-greatest-weakness.

The all-encompassing threat for the South was the intention of the North to destroy the Southern way of life. Explicitly, this basically meant diminishing their political power and influence on a national level, which included abolishing long-standing social structures based on power and importance, farming and rural economies, and reliance on slave labor. With Abraham Lincoln being elected as president in 1860, this only exacerbated the Southern states' fears. Lincoln was viewed as a president who was antislavery and invested principally in Northern interests. The Southern states were consumed with fighting lone battles against the North to protect and preserve singular values, and this was precisely how General Lee approached the fight on the battlefield. Seduced by deeply held beliefs regarding frontal and tactical assaults thought to achieve decisive results in his favor, Lee accomplished no operational or strategic gain.

However, one of the greatest tactical mistakes committed during the American Civil War by the Southern states and General Robert E. Lee impeded the ability to understand the big picture. The mistake made by both the South and General Lee was that neither invested the time to know the ideology that truthfully energized the North. Neither invested time to grasp how the North's pursuit of defeating any movement toward secession basically lacked any moral mandate. This pursuit by the North was fueled by impoverishment that deceitfully claimed righteousness and principled lead intent while at the same time fortifying a wicked status quo. Had this tactical investment taken place, the Southern states and Lee would have realized they had little to fear, little to lose, and much to gain in terms of broadening a fraternity of uniformity.

Time spent to understand the similarities each side shared with one another and the North's underlying motive to crush efforts to secede from the Union would have been far more beneficial for the combatant states. The absurdity of white men who shared the same beliefs of entitlement fighting and killing one another would have never occurred. Discovering consistency with respect to cultural, gender, and racial values would have been advantageous to the warring states, especially the South. One benefit to understanding the bigger picture would have been the opportunity to avoid the death of thousands of Confederate soldiers' lives. Rather than investing time in overreacting to what originally appeared to be real threats to their way of life, there can be no question as to the advisability of this choice.

Discovery would have also disclosed significant information that would explain the North's obsession with unification. Consolidating the states was the Union's commitment to strengthen Thomas Jefferson's legacy, which would advance his vision regarding American exceptionalism. With a unified Union, Jefferson's Empire of Liberty would be a model and a beacon of democracy and freedom to the world. The Founding Fathers' intention for the unified Union was to also be recognized for diplomacy, material resources, innovation, industrialization, individualism, self-government, freedom, and righteousness. Industrialization would certainly help the Southern states to recalibrate their labor force and fine-tune the production of cotton and tobacco and its overall agricultural economy. Prior to the Civil War, the agricultural economy in the South received a boost in terms of credibility regarding Thomas Jefferson's personal appreciation for farming and the Southern states' rural districts.

Another revelation that would help the South to grasp the similarities shared with the North would be the discovery that Ivy League schools such as Harvard University, Yale University, Brown University, Columbia University, and the University of Pennsylvania had been built with donated slave trade money in varied amounts. The North and South shared the same passion and conviction pertaining to the lack of credibility, relevance, and value regarding the Black race. Just as important, the discovery would also have exposed a significant similarity shared between the Southern and Northern states. The South would have come to understand and appreciate Thomas Jefferson's vision regarding American exceptionalism.

The appreciation would come in the form of Jefferson validating the Southern states' cultural and racial values. Revisiting coauthors Tucker and Hendrickson, "The Empire of Liberty was to be made up of one people (founded on the confidence of a free and virtuous populace) and dedicated to liberty under republican institutions. There was to be no place here for subjects, only for citizens. This was why, in principle, Negroes could have no permanent position within the palladium of freedom and why, in practice, Indians (and women) as well had to be excluded from it."[76]

Another defining revelation for the Southern states and General Robert E. Lee from the discovery process reveals the degree to which common values were firmly shared with the North. This revelation has to do with both the North and South having established a system of living that teaches the importance of attaining power, authority, and prominence for the purpose of attaining credibility, relevance, and value. The North, just like the South, absolutely refused to incorporate into its system of living a dedicated curriculum to educate individuals to recognize and value their inherent credibility.

A way of life that validates the values and principles of good conduct toward all people that holds in check self-importance and self-indulgence was absolutely absent from both the North and South systems of living. Without the training to recognize and practice qualities of substantive character, this vacuum was instead occupied with behavior indicative of moral impoverishment. This behavior

---

[76] Tucker, *Empire*, 161.

was subsequently demonstrated through practices of gender inequality and racial and ethnic discrimination and injustice, which was symbolic of the emergence of a "will-to-survive" ideology for both the Southern and Northern states. With this particular system of living, there was a limit to defining oneself and developing self-perception that was strictly based on experiences. The South shared this common value with the North, which blinded their ability to grasp the bigger picture of camaraderie and fall under the influence to pursue power, authority, and prominence through warfare.

After careful thought and deliberation, the Southern states and General Robert E. Lee would have come to understand there really were no reasons to pursue secession or go to war against the North. White men fighting against white men with so much in common pertaining to cultural, social, and racial values would quickly come to be seen as an absurdity. Yes, the South would have to give up slave labor and allow for industrialization that would improve their economy. But the Southern states could still maintain their distinct and distinguished hierarchical system where individuals and groups were ranked according to status and authority.

The Southern states could continue to practice a way of life that made it permissible to practice economic, income, housing, and educational disparities, racial discrimination, and gender inequality. The practice of owning slaves would vanish, but there would be former slaves who would remain reliant on the Southern way of life. A number of slaves had become emotionally and mentally dependent on their masters, second-class citizenship, and the inequality associated with the Southern way of life. And even though former slaves would migrate to Northern states, the way of life would be no different. The North also engaged in the practices of economic, income, housing, gender inequality, educational disparities, and racial discrimination.

The final and most meaningful defining revelation for the Southern states would be the nail in the coffin that defined a commonality with the Northern states—one that still threatens this nation with a failure to envision the bigger picture with regard to its existence. This shared commonality has subsequently placed this nation in a position where its populace is to decide whether to morally advance as an inclusive nation or collapse under the weight of impoverishment that generates self-importance and self-indulgence. Chapter 10 will further discuss this inhibiting commonality that is the legacy of our Founding Fathers.

Chapter 10

TIME TO BREAK WITH A HISTORICAL MODEL

*If you stick a knife in my back nine inches
and pull it out six inches, there's no progress.
If you pull it all the way out, that's not progress.
Progress is healing the wound that the blow made.*
—Malcolm X

*Snatching the eternal out of the desperately fleeting
is the great magic trick of human existence.*
—Tennessee Williams

*Many things which cannot be overcome
when they are together
yield themselves up when taken little by little.*
—Quintus Sertorius

The legacy this nation's Founding Fathers left for Americans to struggle with was a democracy and exceptionalism that lacked moral gravitas. Accordingly, what the South, Robert E. Lee, the North, subsequently the West, and the Founding Fathers all shared in common was a failure to grasp the bigger picture in terms of safeguarding America's existence. With this nation, what has been historically misconstrued is a belief America can survive as a civilization minus a viable moral blueprint. With tenacity, a principled foundation inclusive of every individual that recognized and valued human life was omitted during this nation's commencement. This moral blueprint would have acknowledged an individual's inherent credibility that depicted qualities of meritorious character.

Instead, external significance such as economic status, gender, race, ethnicity, religion, and level of education was recognized and valued. The necessity to develop and insert into this system of living a principled foundation that counterbalanced Thomas Jefferson's concept of American exceptionalism was simply viewed as irrelevant. Jefferson's belief that America is distinct and unique was not just intended to apply to material resources, self-government, industrialization, innovation, and individuality.

Thomas Jefferson's Declaration of Independence was designed to speak for landowners, the wealthy, and educated white men, which he considered the cradle of America's exceptionalism. It was his intention to exclude from the pronouncement women, the BIPOC population, the poor, and the non-English speaking populace. Another Founding Father, James Madison, counseled his elite faction against allowing anyone other than the wealthy, landowners, and educated white men to vote. He reiterated to do so would place their specific faction of elite white men in jeopardy of having their power and wealth taken from them by outside factions with less power and wealth.

These explicit examples established by this nation's Founding Fathers confirm personal interest took precedence over an all-inclusive and practical moral blueprint. At the time this precedence occurred, the moral credibility of our nation deteriorated and has further weakened. American involvement in the genocide of indigenous people, the African slave trade market, and the gender inequality practices directed at women at first deteriorated and weakened this nation's credibility. Sadly, these unsavory examples established by this nation's Founding Fathers and continued by ensuing disciples have been duplicated by an unsophisticated populace.

Well into this twenty-first century, there remain Americans who support an ideology that is motivated by an obsession with self-interest devoid of a principled foundation. This ideology is propelled by a tightly packaged self-interest motivated by a fixation on experiencing power, authority, and prominence. The consequence this nation has experienced throughout its history from the use of this ideology is the creation of a cluster of enduring and painful symptoms, which we've discussed at length in these pages: income, economic, gender, educational, and healthcare inequalities; the rights of women to have a dominant voice regarding reproduction issues; systemic and interpersonal racism; unbridled injustice; discrimination; gun violence; addiction; and the diminishing value of human life.

The human-made creation of the aforementioned societal ills historically has been addressed with numerous attempts to resolve the harm inflicted upon various factions of the populace. Governmental, political, civic, and church leaders throughout our history have attempted to resolve these symptoms, which is nothing more than folly. The foolishness is exposed when we understand that legislated laws do nothing more than encourage people to manipulate their behavior and, at the same time, maintain their self-centered ideology. Whereas, if we were to change the hearts and minds of people through an educational process to recognize and practice the best attributes they inherently and personally possess, the behavior would reflect a collective good. It is ironic that society gladly endorses paying athletes millions of dollars to witness what it is reluctant and, at times, refuses to demonstrate: individual success in support of the collective good.

All societal ills represent symptoms arising from an ideology that is driven by self-interest motivated by an obsession to experience power, authority, and prominence. It is true there are varying views with respect to human nature, as there are individuals who believe that seeking an advantage over another person or group is part of that nature. Having said that, if human nature is educated to recognize, value, and practice its inherent credibility representing the best attributes that embody substantive character, the outcome is obvious. Self-interest motivated by an obsession to experience power, authority, and prominence can be displaced with the opening to experience personal empowerment, fulfillment, and completeness.

Again, we can trace America's fascination with this self-interest ideology back to the beginning of this nation with the Founding Fathers. Rest assured, however, that this specific ideology did not begin with this elite group. The ideology that endorses personal interest over the collective good has actually been used by humankind well over the past three thousand years. The Sumerians, recognized as the earliest known civilization in the historical region of Mesopotamia, were well acquainted with this ideology. The opportunity to break from a time-honored and historical mold of placing individual success over the collective good presented itself to this nation at a critical moment in its existence. An opportunity was missed for the development of an all-inclusive and practical moral blueprint at this nation's threshold that would have separated itself from the fate of previously fallen civilizations.

Thomas Jefferson linked American exceptionalism with individualism, which can be a positive trait. However, since the beginning of this nation to this current time period, this worthwhile attribute has been exploited to mean self-interest at the expense of a collective good. Educating the populace to recognize, value, and practice the inherent credibility they bring into this life—that comprises qualities descriptive of substantive character—and individualism will support a collective good and illustrate a genuine form of American exceptionalism. Anytime the collective good supersedes self-interest, that is exceptional.

Another aspect of American exceptionalism is consumerism, which in theory, can be a constructive experience. As with individualism, since the beginning of this nation to this current time period, consumerism has taken on a broader implication. This expanded implication includes an emotional component that has to do with a fixation on pursuing personal happiness and success through materialism. The accumulation of external assets, such as Gucci leather goods, Louie Vuitton luggage and accessories, Hermès silk scarves, Rolex Swiss luxury watches, Prada clothing and accessories, Bentley and Rolls-Royce luxury cars, and Cartier's French high-end jewelry, can offer personal happiness and success, but only up to the time of day another drug of choice is needed to distract from the internal emptiness and sorrow.

As one of seven advanced world economies, America has a conspicuous income inequality. Middle- to lower-income factions of the populace can be heard complaining about how they are struggling to live from paycheck to paycheck. Visible poverty and homelessness can be observed throughout urban America. It is logical there would be individuals who would pursue their happiness and success through power, authority, and prominence gained by preserving this inequality.

It is also logical that individuals negatively impacted by income inequality would pursue happiness and success through obsessive consumerism—accumulating excessive debt to distract from an internal emptiness and sorrow. With both sides of this equation deficient in recognizing their innate qualities that represent a bonafide credibility, relevance, and wholeness, consumerism and materialism become pacifiers for the impoverished. It is true—consumerism and materialism can be healthy components of American exceptionalism as long as its populace first learns that happiness and success are based on an acceptance that personal legitimacy is initiated from within, never externally derived.

When American exceptionalism is limited to self-government, individualism, and material resources, while ignoring an expansion to include the collective good, the consequence is tragic. Mimicking the stock exchange on a bad day, the value of human life will continue to spiral downward. This fixation on experiencing power, authority, and prominence in pursuit of limited exceptionalism encourages the impoverished to take advantage of vulnerable Americans. Precious human lives, such as innocent schoolchildren, college students, and harmless adults, become revolting statistics under the heading of mass killings.

What is magnified by this behavior is a perverted exceptionalism antagonistic toward the collective good. Gun ownership champions this wicked form of American exceptionalism, primarily for those who value their own lives and safety over the safety of those who could be harmed by their weapons. Amplifying the need to develop an excessive pride when experiencing self-government and individualism helps to promote the need for automatic weapons and an excessive stockpile to wield more power. According to the Switzerland-based Small Arms Survey (SAS), which is accepted as a valued international source for unbiased and dependable information pertaining to small arms, "the United States is the only nation in the world where civilian guns outnumber people. There are 120 guns for every 100 Americans."[77]

Living within a nation that has more guns than citizens helps to strengthen this excessive pride. Developing reasonable gun control measures without first teaching the masses to recognize and value qualities comprising inherent credibility will never come to fruition against what, on the surface, appears to be impenetrable self-interest.

For various Americans, unanticipated are the fierce and painful episodes of depression, suicidal thoughts, alcoholism, drug addiction, and other severe mental health issues. When an individual lacks a personal moral blueprint that exemplifies meritorious qualities of character, problems affecting mental health can surface. The blueprint allows a person to expand their perception of oneself beyond being solely influenced by positive or negative experiences. To give into developing an overinflated or under-inflated self-perception primarily as a result of experiences sets up the possibility of encountering a social interchange that can leave a person feeling disenfranchised.

The disconnectedness is due to the failure to experience personal fulfillment as promised by a system of living that insists credibility, relevance, and value are derived from external factors. This promise originates from a system that fails to educate its populace to recognize and value qualities demonstrative of substantive character as reflective of a person's inherent credibility. The absence of a moral blueprint leaves a person with only power, authority, and prominence to achieve an insubstantial and unstable fulfillment. With that in mind, feeling disenfranchised or enfranchised, which results

---

[77] Kara Fox, et al, "How US Gun Culture Stacks Up with the Rest of the World," *CNN.com*, April 10, 2023, https://www.cnn.com/2021/11/26/world/us-gun-culture-world-comparison-intl-cmd/index.html.

in developing an overinflated or under-inflated self-perception, is the accomplished goal of betrayal, rejection, abuse, and corruption.

It is ironic that the type of exceptionalism Jefferson promoted had its focus on external factors that lacked a developed all-inclusive blueprint expressive of substantive qualities of character. As a consequence of this undeveloped integral component of individuality, this nation's moral growth was restricted from the beginning of its existence. And well into the twenty-first century, America remains committed to adhering to this legacy of self-interest. The sad commentary linked to the legacy is that America now qualifies as a civilization in a moral quagmire moving toward collapse. The checklist of potential causes that can contribute to this collapse deserves serious concern.

This pattern of decline is inching our nation closer and closer toward a collision course with an unforgiving fate due to the absence of an all-inclusive moral blueprint and evidenced in the current breakdown, including social cohesion and a bitterly divided populace; political instability, congressional infighting, corruption, and a Supreme Court in moral disarray; special interest overshadowing a collective good; economic inequality; gender inequality and women losing their autonomy; racism and internal racism intensifying; escalating rates of depression, suicide, alcoholism, and drug addiction among younger adults; poverty, homelessness, and crime worsening; immigration issues amplified at the southern border; and mounting climate concerns. This is the same collision course many preceding civilizations collapsed under when self-importance and self-indulgence, with the primary focus on materialism, power, and authority, dominated a system of living.

Another symptom representing a pattern of decline was the attack on the United States Capitol Building in Washington, DC, on

January 6, 2021, by a mob who sought to keep former US President Donald Trump in power by prohibiting Congress from counting the Electoral College votes that would finalize the victory of President-elect Joe Biden. This blatant act to overthrow democracy in favor of installing an autocrat as president was resounding evidence America was and is in a downward spiral. This unambiguous act was an attempt to duplicate the Founding Fathers' example when personal interest took precedence over moral authority and the collective good. In his bid to become the forty-fifth president of the United States from 2017 to 2021, former President Donald Trump adopted a platform slogan, "Make America Great Again."

To this day, "Make America Great Again" remains his catch-phrase, as well as in the minds of his followers. For a number of Americans, this nation was once at its greatest when the wealthy and power brokers representing a bloc of the white populace dominated the economic, government, political, social, religious, and educational sectors throughout America. This group of people, including former President Donald Trump, believe themselves to be the rightful successors of the Founding Fathers' example of establishing power, authority, and prominence.

To bolster this mentality of entitlement, certain teachings that emerged during the intellectual movement known as the Age of Enlightenment or The age of reason (1685–1815) became popular by calling attention to the use of reason to understand life on this plane of existence. Popular then and well into the future were philosophers such as John Locke, Voltaire, and Montesquieu, who brought new and sweeping ideas to a system of living regarding individual liberty, religious tolerance, and separation of powers. The same would be true for the work of other philosophers, such as Jean-Jacques Rousseau's "Social Contract" and Adam Smith's "The Wealth of

Nations." However, no one would be more in the spotlight of notoriety than the acclaimed and prominent German physician, naturalist, and anthropologist Johann Friedrich Blumenbach. The esteemed naturalist was recognized for making significant contributions to the field of anthropology by studying various human varieties based on physical characteristics such as skin color, skull, and facial features. Approximately sixty male craniums were used for purposes of measurement, comparison, and classification.[78]

At the height of Blumenbach's research, he separated humankind into five variations. Shortly following his discovery, the term *race* was used to categorize different human populations. The five races were subsequently listed in order of importance and beauty. This type of systematic cataloging reflected Blumenbach's personal biases, elitism, and impoverishment regarding an individual's inherent credibility. An excellent example to illustrate a collective good would have been to abandon listing the races based on his biases pertaining to physical characteristics that minimized the credibility of people not Caucasian.

Nonetheless, at the top of the list was the Caucasian or white race (Europeans, Middle Easterners, and South Asians). The term "Caucasian" was used to refer to the people residing in the Caucasus region between the Black Sea and the Caspian Sea. The region mainly comprised Armenia, Azerbaijan, Georgia, and parts of Southern Russia, which included the Caucasus Mountains. As a natural barrier between Eastern Europe and Western Asia, this region was believed to be, in Blumenbach's thinking, an archetype of beauty and nobility.

Blumenbach provides further clarification in his book titled *The Anthropological Treatises of Johann Friedrich Blumenbach*, which includes

---

[78] Johann Friedrich Blumenbach, *The Anthropological Treatises of Johann Friedrich Blumenbach* (London: The Anthropological Society, 1895).

the first (1775) and third editions (1795) of the published *On the Natural Variety of Mankind*. Blumenbach states:

> Caucasian variety. I have taken the name of this variety from Mount Caucasus, both because its neighborhood, and especially its southern slope, produces the most beautiful race of men, I mean the Georgian; and because all physiological reasons converge to this, that in that region, if anywhere, it seems we ought with the greatest probability to place the autochthones of mankind. For in the first place, that stock displays, as we have seen, the most beautiful form of the skull, from which, as from a mean and primeval type.

> The others diverge by most easy gradations on both sides to the two ultimate extremes (that is, on the one side the Mongolian, on the other the Ethiopian). Besides, it is white in color, which we may fairly assume to have been the primitive color of mankind, since, as we have shown above, it is very easy for that to degenerate into brown, but very much more difficult for dark to become white, when the secretion and precipitation of this carbonaceous pigment has once deeply struck root.[79]

Following the Caucasian or white race were the Mongolian or yellow race (including all East Asians), Malayan or brown race (including Southeast Asians and Pacific Islanders), Ethiopian or Black race (including all sub-Saharan Africans), and American or red race

---

[79] Johann Friedrich Blumenbach, *The Anthropological Treatises of Johann Friedrich Blumenbach* (London, UK: The Anthropological Society, 1865), 269.

(including all Native Americans). Solid scientific research and discovery were manipulated to propel self-interest into positions of power, authority, and prominence. Had Blumenbach's research findings remained neutral and absent of personal judgments, race superiority and inferiority would not have become issues that continued to intensely divide America throughout its existence. The Atlantic Slave Trade began in 1526 and concluded approximately in 1867, with roughly 10.7 million captured men, women, and children arriving in the Americas.

The disservice Blumenbach provided the global community was to immortalize the practices of discrimination and injustice based on national differences in the form and color of the human body. It is easy to understand Blumenbach's motives since he was a product of a system of living devoid of an educational agenda to teach a person to recognize, value, and practice qualities of exemplary character that represent an individual's inherent credibility.

It was imperative that Blumenbach achieve some form of scientific legitimacy and personal fulfillment from external sources, such as his culture and professional community. Since he was unaware of his inherent credibility, focusing on cultural superiority and racial ranking diverted his attention from his own intellectual, emotional, and spiritual impoverishment. Again, Blumenbach needed to produce biased research that established the idea that one race of humanity was superior to all others, which is a recipe to pursue power, authority, and prominence by any means necessary.

The editor's preface written by an official of King's College, Cambridge, on January 1, 1865, for the book, *The Anthropological Treatises* includes the following:

> Of the five races there are three which he considers
> above all as the principal races; and therefore, he deals
> with those first. These are the Caucasian, which is not

only for Blumenbach the most beautiful, and that to which the pre-eminence belongs, but the primitive race; then, the Mongolian and Ethiopian, in which the author sees the extreme degenerations of the human species.

As to the other races, they are only for Blumenbach, transitional: that is, the American is the passage from the Caucasian to the Mongolian; and the Malay, from the Caucasian to the Ethiopian. These two races are put off till the last instead of being treated intermediately, as they ought to be, if they were not considered as divisions of an inferior rank.[80]

In Blumenbach's words in *The Anthropological Treatises*, he justifies the decision to rank the Caucasian (white) variety above all other varieties. He states:

After a long and attentive consideration, all mankind, as far as it is at present known to us, seems to me as if it may best, according to natural truth, be divided into the five following varieties, which may be designated and distinguished from each other by the names Caucasian, Mongolian, Ethiopian, American, and Malay. I have allotted the first place to the Caucasian, for the reasons given below, which make me esteem it the primeval one.

Caucasian variety. Color white, cheeks rosy; hair brown or chestnut-colored; head subglobular; face oval, straight, its parts moderately defined, forehead

---

[80] Blumenbach, *Treatises*, xi.

smooth, nose narrow, slightly hooked, mouth small. The primary teeth placed perpendicularly to each jaw; the lips (especially the lower one) moderately open, the chin full and rounded. In general, that kind of appearance which, according to our opinion of symmetry, we consider most handsome and becoming. To this first variety belong the inhabitants of Europe (except the Lapps and the remaining descendants of the Finns) and those of Eastern Asia, as far as the river Obi, the Caspian Sea, and the Ganges; and lastly, those of Northern Africa.[81]

There is no documented evidence that Blumenbach had any direct contact with America's Founding Fathers. However, it is a safe assumption that Blumenbach's ideas and writings had a significant influence on their thinking about race and human diversity. The renowned American paleontologist, biologist, historian, and author Stephen Jay Gould states in his book, *The Mismeasure of Man*:

> Blumenbach first presented his work *On the Natural Variety of Mankind* as a doctoral dissertation to the medical faculty of the University of Gottingen in Germany in 1775, as the minutemen of Lexington and Concord began the American Revolution. He then republished the text for general distribution in 1776, as a fateful meeting in Philadelphia proclaimed our independence.
>
> The coincidence of three great documents in 1776-Jefferson's Declaration of Independence (on

---

[81] Blumenbach, *Treatises*, 264–265.

the politics of liberty), Adam Smith's *Wealth of Nations* (on the economics of individualism), and Blumenbach's treatise on racial classification (on the science of human diversity)-records the social ferment of these decades, and sets the wider context that makes Blumenbach's taxonomy, and his decision to call the European race Caucasian, so important for our history and current concerns.[82]

Blumenbach was the least racist, most egalitarian, and most genial of all Enlightenment writers on the subject of human diversity. How peculiar that the man most committed to human unity and to inconsequential moral and intellectual differences among groups should have changed the mental geometry of human order to a scheme that has promoted conventional racism ever since. Yet, on second thought, this situation is really not so peculiar or unusual, for most scientists have always been unaware of the mental machinery, and particularly of the visual or geometric implications, behind all theorizing.[83]

Blumenbach lived in an age when ideas of progress, and of the cultural superiority of European life, dominated the political and social world of his contemporaries. Implicit and loosely formulated (or even unconscious) notions of racial ranking fit well with

---

[82] Stephen Jay Gould, *The Mismeasure of Man*, (New York: Norton, 1981), 401–402.

[83] Gould, *Mismeasure*, 405–406.

such a worldview. In changing the geometry of human order to a system of ranking by worth, I doubt that Blumenbach did anything consciously in the overt service of racism. I think that he was only, and largely passively, recording the pervasive social view of his time. But ideas have consequences, whatever the motives or intentions of their promoters.[84]

Stephen Jay Gould expresses a sympathetic point of view for Blumenbach and rationalization for his racial classification. The excuses, "the least racist, most egalitarian, living in an age of the cultural superiority of European life," are similar to the sympathetic points of view expressed in support of America's Founding Fathers. The wealthy and powerful men during this nation's commencement were living in an age of the cultural superiority of male Caucasian life. Racial injustice, gender inequality, and intolerance for the poor dominated the cultural landscape. What dominated Blumenbach's culture was the same impoverishment that dominated the cultural landscape of the Founding Fathers. What was quite discernible for both cultures was the absence of a moral blueprint designed to develop and protect the political and social lives of a populace different from the male Caucasian.

This system of living just described for America was in lock-step with the influential thinkers of the Enlightenment Age. Jamelle Bouie, a columnist for the *New York Times* and political analyst for CBS News, has written extensively about the significant influence Enlightenment thinkers had on America's Founding Fathers and the creation of its racial rationale. In his June 5, 2018, *Slate.com* article titled "The Enlightenment's Dark Side: How the Enlightenment

---

[84] Gould, *Mismeasure*, 406.

Created Modern Race Thinking, and Why We Should Confront It," Bouie states:

> The Enlightenment is a straightforward story of progress, with major currents like race and colonialism cast aside, if they are acknowledged at all. Divorced from its cultural and historical context, this "Enlightenment" acts as an ideological talisman, less to do with contesting ideas or understanding history, and more to do with identity. It's a standard, meant to distinguish its holders for their commitment to "rationalism" and "classical liberalism."
>
> But even as they venerate the Enlightenment, these writers actually underestimate its influence on the modern world. At its heart, the movement contained a paradox: Ideas of human freedom and individual rights took root in nations that held other human beings in bondage and were then in the process of exterminating native populations. Colonial domination and expropriation marched hand in hand with the spread of "liberty," and liberalism arose alongside our modern notions of race and racism.
>
> These weren't incidental developments or the mere remnants of earlier prejudice. Race as we understand it—a biological taxonomy that turns physical difference into relations of domination—is a product of the Enlightenment. Racism as we understand it now, as a socio-political order based on the permanent

hierarchy of particular groups, developed as an attempt to resolve the fundamental contradiction between professing liberty and upholding slavery.

But it took the scientific thought of the Enlightenment to create an enduring racial taxonomy and the "color-coded, white-over-black" ideology with which we are familiar. Johann Friedrich Blumenbach's influential 1776 volume On the Natural Varieties of Mankind posited five divisions of humanity, beginning with "Caucasians." These frameworks evolved into theories of racial difference, developed to square a conceptual circle. If natural rights are universal—if everyone has the capacity to reason—then what is the explanation for enslaved Africans or "savages" in the Americas, who do not seem to act and reason like white Europeans? The answer is biological inferiority, in accordance with those racial classifications.

We still live in a world shaped by Enlightenment ideas of race and white supremacy. These notions of inherent inferiority still hold purchase in our society. And political liberalism is still too compatible with both. The path to a truly universal liberalism—one that can actually liberate—demands that we grapple with its ugly heritage. To confront the paradox of the Enlightenment is to take its values seriously; to dismiss it is to prefer hagiography to truth.[85]

---

[85] Jamelle Bouie, "The Enlightenment's Dark Side: How the Enlightenment Created Modern Race Thinking, and Why We Should Confront It," Slate.com, June 5, 2018, https://slate.com/news-and-politics/2018/06/taking-the-enlightenment-seriously-requires-talking-about-race.html.

Nicholas E. Magnis captured the level of racial superiority in his article titled "Thomas Jefferson and Slavery: An Analysis of His Racist Thinking as Revealed by His Writings and Political Behavior." Magnis states:

> Thomas Jefferson believed fervently that all persons of African descent should not be permitted to reside in the new republic unless they were enslaved. Throughout his life, Jefferson maintained that if freed, the former slaves must be colonized outside of North America to Africa or the Caribbean Islands. He based this imperative on his belief that the Blacks "are inferior to the whites in the endowments both of body and mind" (Jefferson, 1787/1954, p. 143).

> A review of Jefferson's major published work, *Notes on the State of Virginia* (1787/1954), indicates that Jefferson was not rational and scientific when he wrote of the African-descended slaves in Virginia. His conclusion, developed in his book that the slaves were inferior in body and mind resulted from thinking that was extremely emotional and illogical. Jefferson broke with the prevailing Enlightenment thought when he speculated on the causes for what he believed was the innate inferiority of the Black race. In addition, soon after writing the Declaration of Independence, Jefferson participated in political activity that clearly indicated his unwavering belief that Blacks, if emancipated, must not live as freemen in Virginia.

> Lastly, a consummate political strategist, Jefferson did almost nothing to advance abolition during his forty years in the turbulent political arena of Virginia and

the new republic. The singular positive measure that he advocated in 1784 to prevent slavery from flourishing in the new states of the northwest territory he diametrically opposed in 1820, when his desire to prevent the dissolution of the Union over the issue of the spread of slavery became more important for him than the curtailment of slavery.[86]

In the place of a moral blueprint was a blueprint designed to develop and protect self-importance and self-indulgence, motivated by the self-interest to safeguard the male Caucasian. Rather than Blumenbach using his investigative and scientific skills to highlight an inherent credibility that bonds humankind to one another, the focus was to identify external differences and a hierarchical race pyramid. Division and superiority became the standard of measure for Blumenbach. This division took precedence rather than creating a comprehensive study that identified the different physical variations of mankind to highlight the gifts of uniqueness and the commonality that each group shared with one another. It is of little comfort to this nation and the global community that Blumenbach's racial hierarchical classification received criticism as scientifically inaccurate and personally biased; the damage to creating a cohesive national and global community had commenced.

Raj Bhopal, emeritus professor of public health, Univeristy of Edinburgh retired staff, dean of molecular, genetic and population health sciences, captures the spirit of the criticism in his article titled "The Beautiful Skull and Blumenbach's Errors: The Birth of the Scientific Concept of Race." He states:

---

[86] Nicholas E. Magnis, "Thomas Jefferson and Slavery: An Analysis of His Racist Thinking as Revealed by His Writings and Political Behavior," JSTOR, *Journal of Black Studies*, Vol. 29, No. 4, Mar 1999, 491–509, https://www.jstor.org/stable/2645866.

Mostly, Blumenbach's writing retained a scientific stance, but he exposed his bias on beauty when he wrote that the Caucasian skull of a Georgian female was the "most handsome and becoming." He stated that the most beautiful people live in the southern slope of Mount Caucasus—that is, the Georgian people. He then speculated on the origins of humans and made his second error, by going beyond the available evidence. Blumenbach states, "We may fairly assume to have been the primitive color of mankind." His reasoning was that it is easy to change from white to brown but not vice versa. Time has shown that this view was wrong.

Blumenbach's work was a turning point in the history of race and science, although it was nearly 200 years before the lessons were properly absorbed. Blumenbach's legacy is tarnished by biases and errors, and it teaches us that even great scientists can be led astray by personal views (such as notions about beauty) shaped by the ethos of their times. His original words also show how the simple, clear-cut classification of five distinct human races displaced the complex reality of gradations and the unity of humanity (including equal potential). Blumenbach's name has been associated with scientific racism, but his arguments actually undermined racism. Blumenbach could not have foreseen the coming abuse of his ideas and classification in the nineteenth and (first half of the) twentieth centuries.

We continue to struggle with the complexity of the concepts of race and ethnicity, and the resultant imperfect classifications, in our multi-ethnic world. Now, Blumenbach's varieties of humanity can be seen in virtually every major city, and through the visual media globally. Blumenbach's thinking, despite its faults, continues to be relevant, inspiring, and illuminating.[87]

Nell Irvin Painter proclaims on the book cover of her publication *The History of White People*:

Our story begins in Greek and Roman antiquity, where the concept of race did not exist, only geography and the opportunity to conquer and enslave others. Not until the eighteenth century did an obsession with whiteness flourish, with the German invention of the notion of Caucasian beauty and virtue. This theory made northern Europeans into "Saxons," "Anglo-Saxons," and "Teutons" (an ancient northern European tribe), envisioned as uniquely handsome natural rulers. Here was a worldview congenial to northern Europeans bent on empire.

There followed an explosion of theories of race, now focusing on racial temperament as well as skin color. Its chief spokesman, Ralph Waldo Emerson, did the most to label Anglo-Saxons – icons of beauty and

---

[87] Raj Bhopal, "The Beautiful Skull and Blumenbach's Errors: The Birth of the Scientific Concept of Race," *BMJ 2007; 335:1308,*https://www.researchgate.net/publication/5693470_The_beautiful_skull_and_Blumenbach%27s_errors_The_birth_of_the_scientific_concept_of_race.

virtue – as the only true Americans. It was an ideal that excluded not only blacks, but also all ethnic groups not of Protestant, northern European background. The Irish and Native Americans were out and, later, so were the Chinese, Jews, Italians, Slavs, and Greeks – all deemed racially alien.[88]

Nell Irvin Painter continues:

Were there "white" people in antiquity? Certainly, some assume so, as though categories we use today could be read backwards over the millennia. People with light skin certainly existed well before our own times. But did anyone think they were "white" or that their character related to their color? No, for neither the idea of race nor the idea of "white" people had been invented, and people's skin color did not carry useful meaning. What mattered was where they lived; were their lands damp or dry; were they virile or prone to impotence, hard or soft; could they be seduced by the luxuries of civilized society or were they warriors through and through? What were their habits of life? Rather than as "white" people, northern Europeans were known by vague tribal names: Scythians and Celts, then Gauls and Germani.

Thus, we must sift through the intellectual history Americans claim as Westerners keeping in mind that long before science dictated the terms of human differences as "race," long before racial scientists began

---

[88] Nell Irvin Painter, The History of White People (New York: W.W. Norton & Company, 2011).

to measure heads and concoct racial theory, ancient Greeks and Romans had their own means of describing the peoples of their world as they knew it more than two millennia ago. And inevitably, the earliest accounts of our story are told from on high, by rulers dominant at a particular time. Power affixes the markers of history.[89]

The only viable response, at the present time, for the knock at the door of American civilization is a candid and forthright American exceptionalism that is inclusive of all its populace. Deserved recognition of the multicultural society this nation exemplifies is a suitable counter for this type of rousing. The knock is a serious wake-up call that requires the fullest attention of this diverse community. A new and indisputable enlightenment age presents itself that will be an addendum to the limited concept of exceptionalism this nation's Founding Fathers initially established for America.

Their original conception of exceptionalism lacked the vision of a bigger picture for America that included a moral blueprint representative of this diverse nation. With the Founding Fathers solely focused on establishing credibility, relevance, and value based on the attainment of external ambitions, such as self-government, material resources, industrialization, innovation, and individualism, one discernible context was disclosed. The Founding Fathers possessed a limited vision pertaining to credibility, relevance, and value, which was revealed by the lack of developed personal moral blueprints. Due to this shortcoming, accomplishing goals for the collective good was over overshadowed by self-interest.

The time has arrived for America to move morally beyond the limited achievement of its Founding Fathers. What escaped the thinking

---

[89] Painter, *The History*, 1–2.

of this elite group of men was an understanding of America's bigger picture, which needed to include a landscape favoring an ethical structure. A multicultural America would prosper by being ethically enriched by teachings that make clear personal credibility, relevance, and value reach far beyond the attainment of power, authority, and prominence, primarily through external aspirations. To avoid falling into intellectual, emotional, and spiritual impoverishment by viewing one another with differences as obstacles to experiencing "certain unalienable rights, that among these are life, liberty, and the pursuit of happiness," learning how to achieve personal empowerment, rather than vain power, would help America to adapt to a bigger ethically structured picture.

The antagonist that is inducing the serious knock at the door is not any particular race, political party, politician, corporation, technology, individual, religion, social curriculum, drug, or far right/left group. The antagonist is a three-thousand-year-old system of living that has survived by being successfully passed down from generation to generation. No cultural authorization has historically existed to counterbalance its objective. The aim of this specific system of living is to undervalue the importance of educating an individual to recognize, value, and practice the best virtues a person enters this life inherently possessing. What makes this scandalous act so dangerous is that a person is fleeced of the opportunity to develop qualities that exemplify their admirable character and experience authentic credibility and relevance.

In its place, the system encourages a person to pursue a fragile form of credibility and relevance primarily through external sources. We've covered the numerous problems that occur with this approach at length in this text, but one significant problem that emerges is the exposure to power, authority, and manipulation from others who have formerly achieved a measure of credibility and relevance. Hence, the birth of injustice, bigotry, gender inequality, discrimination, the banning of books, and woke rhetoric. Another notable problem that emerges is the dependency that develops on external sources for validation regarding personal credibility, relevance, and value. Both issues inhibit the personal development of autonomy, individuality, community, empathy, and critical thinking.

Because this three-thousand-year-old system of living is based solely on the attainment and use of power, authority, and prominence to attain credibility and relevance, the serious knock at the door represents a malicious intent to discredit or destroy. This antagonist is a vital contributor to the collapse of once powerful and dominant civilizations. Internally configured to eventually collapse from within is any system of living representative of relationships that lacks a dedicated commitment to establishing a way of life buoyed by principled morality.

Revisiting the disservice Blumenbach bestowed upon the global community was to ratify and validate the appropriateness of building an empire rather than cultivate coalitions of equal worth. The creation of a hierarchal race classification was the result of Blumenbach's limited understanding of his own inherent credibility. His hierarchal race classification provided the inspiration for humanity to continue their misguided commitment to establishing a ranking way of life pertaining to relationships and pursuing the top of the power, authority, and prominence pyramid.

Failing to educate an individual to their inherent attributes of legitimacy translates into a lost opportunity to develop honorable character. The importance of developing substantive character cannot be overstated. It is this lion's share of personal growth that enables a person to hear, see, and capture their own essence, as well as another person or group. Lacking this opportunity for personal growth leaves an individual to be consumed with their own self-importance and self-indulgence, which is revealed as narcissistic and impoverished.

The lion's share of personal growth is lost, and the ability to hear, see, and capture the essence of oneself or another person or group is of no concern; the need to be right is all that matters. There is a limit to an individual's options for defining oneself and developing self-perception. Unaware of attributes comprising inherent credibility, an individual tends to use positive or negative experiences to define oneself. Without an appreciation of one's inherent character, an individual cannot apply their enduring qualities to separate from experiences and, more importantly, they cannot internalize the encounters on a personal level when processing the experiences.

The antagonist would want nothing more than for America to collapse from within under the weight of a morally broken society. Fractured and divided as this nation currently is economically, socially, politically, racially, and academically, this is the exact moment in American history when it is appropriate to trust the confession. This nation has reached a critical moment in its evolution when understanding the importance of living one's life based on an inherent credibility is essential to its continuance. Relying heavily on limited concepts of exceptionalism, such as self-government, material resources, industrialization, innovation, and individuality, has nearly brought this nation to its knees due to a lack of an all-inclusive moral blueprint.

To disavow this ignorance of a moral awareness that exemplifies the best personal attributes acknowledges an exceptionalism that promotes and advances personal freedom to any American willing to save this nation from being preoccupied with self-interest. The development of admirable character supports the dream of bringing this multicultural community to epitomize a people united together by reason of a literal moral blueprint rather than a theoretical design.

The moment is at hand when the statement made by a wise person makes the most sense: "If you bring forth what is within you, what you bring will save you. If you do not bring forth what is within you, what you do not bring forth will destroy you."[90] It is time to demonstrate to one another and the rest of the global community what real exceptionalism looks, feels, and lives like.

At the beginning of this chapter, only the first part of the Malcolm X statement is quoted. The second part of his statement is as follows: "Progress is healing the wound that the blow made. They haven't pulled the knife out; they won't even admit that it's there." Progress is healing from the intellectual, emotional, and spiritual impoverishment that motivated the blow. This progress also involves education to accept the best qualities innately bestowed upon oneself, as well as on every individual entering this life. The final solution discloses there is no need to wait for an admittance of wrongdoing when the embrace of substantive character is the healing agent.

---

90 Elaine Pagels, *Beyond Belief: The Secret Gospel of Thomas* (New York: Random House Vintage Books, 2003), 32.

ABOUT THE AUTHOR

Lorenzo D. Leonard is a writer and thought leader who is committed to resolving societal problems by addressing the root cause of the social symptoms of injustice, oppression, gender inequality, racism, classism, and ageism through his work.

The deep insights and challenging rhetoric in *Trust the Confession* seek to deepen understanding, prompt reflection, and provide a clarion call for meaningful and lasting change.

His previous works include The True Holy War (2009), Empires vs. Coalitions (2013), At First Glance (2021), Rules of Engagement (2021), and To the Issue of Credibility, Relevance, and Value: Educate to Character (2022).